HUNTED

The true story of outlaw Mike Donnelly and his sidekicks, whose history of crime and punishment in the Pacific Northwest—including the murder of William Crisp at Hope, Idaho, in 1923—spanned a period of forty years.

Dale Selle

Bonner County Historical Society, Inc.
Sandpoint, Idaho

Published by:
Bonner County Historical Society
611 South Ella Avenue
Sandpoint, Idaho 83864
(208) 263-2344
www.bonnercountyhistory.org

Printed in the United States of America by Caxton Printers of Caldwell, Idaho.

Cover design and maps: Mike Dixon, Rastrographics
Interior design and composition: Ann Ferguson

Cover images:
Booking photograph of Mike Donnelly. Photograph courtesy of the Idaho State Historical Society in Boise, Idaho.

Hope, Idaho, in the summer of 1923. Bonner County Historical Society photograph.

Spokane Daily Chronicle [Spokane, Washington] July 18, 1923.

Photograph of Dale Selle courtesy of Patricia Selle.

First Edition

ISBN-10: 0985055405
ISBN-13: 978-0-9850554-0-0

To my cousin Lowell Messman.

Thanks for helping with research
in northwestern Washington.

Contents

Illustrations

viii

Maps

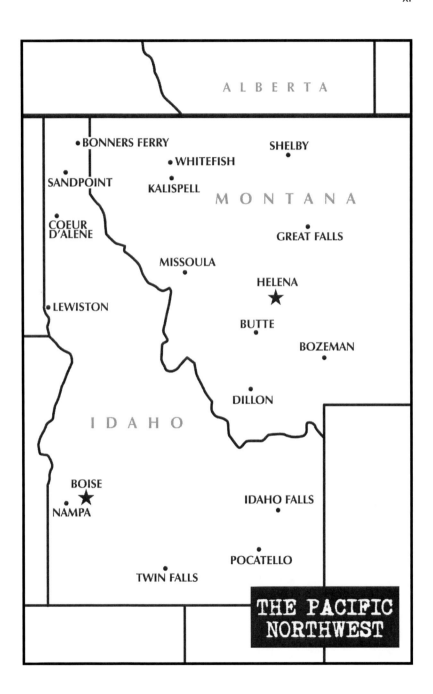

Foreword

When I was a boy of nine or ten years of age, my Uncle Dalton Hawkins showed his son Will and me some holes in the decking of an old wooden bridge that crossed the Pack River, about a mile north of the present Highway 200 bridge in Bonner County, Idaho. Dalton said they were bullet holes, put there by members of a sheriff's posse, shooting at two men who robbed and murdered a storeowner in Hope, Idaho, in the 1920s. Will and I were told that our grandfather, William Edward Hawkins, was a member of the posse that pursued these murderers and brought them to justice. Such a story, of course, fascinated boys our age.

As an adult, I decided that I would like to know more about what actually happened back then. The more that I read the old newspaper accounts of the story, the more interesting this bit of local history turned out to be. I thought others might also like to know what I discovered. In this book, I not only recount the events surrounding the Hope shooting, but also tell the colorful history of "gun play" in the lives of the two men who committed that crime.

Records are sketchy, and none of the participants are still living to relate what happened early in these men's careers. Max C. King wrote a feature article published in the "Charmed Land Magazine" of *The Seattle Sunday Times*, March 10, 1963, for which he located and interviewed a few aging witnesses to one of the outlaw's earlier escapades in western Washington, and I drew on these comments for this book.

Many facts reported in this story came from official documents. Other descriptions of events are speculative and conjectural, extrapolated from the facts. For most of the story, however, I relied upon interviews of witnesses done by newspaper reporters, as well as newspaper accounts published during the time that the drama was unfolding. These various newspaper reporters deserve credit for most descriptions of events retold in *Hunted*. To avoid interrupting the flow of the story, individual newspaper citations are not included. A list of the newspapers from which the story was taken can be found in the bibliography.

This is not a scholarly work. It is a story based on facts, but everyone knows that newspaper articles are not always entirely accurate and "the facts" in this case were sometimes reported differently in different newspapers. Some of the articles from which this story was gleaned contradicted other articles. I have chosen the newspaper "facts" that best fit the story. Errors published in the original newspaper stories have undoubtedly been repeated in this version of the tale. Nevertheless, the newspaper reporters surely had the basic information correct, and while the details may not be one hundred percent accurate, *Hunted* portrays things mostly as they really happened

Prologue

Near the end of May 1923, two paroled convicts from the Washington State Penitentiary in Walla Walla got together in Spokane, Washington, and became "partners in crime." One of these men was thirty-nine-year-old Mike Donnelly, newly paroled after serving twelve years of a life sentence for second-degree murder. The other man was thirty-one-year-old Noah Arnold, also paroled after serving five years of a maximum twenty-year sentence for manslaughter. Neither man in this pair had a single ounce of respect for the law.

Both ex-cons were already in violation of the conditions of their parole agreements for failing to report to their parole officers. The pair had further violated parole by arming themselves with revolvers and leaving the state of Washington. With packsacks full of camping gear and provisions, they stowed away on an eastbound freight train.

These reckless fugitives were about to embark on a two-month crime spree in Idaho and Montana. Their string of holdups ended in Bonner County, Idaho, with the fatal shooting of one of their many robbery victims.

Both men came to the fateful summer of 1923 carrying a great deal of criminal baggage. One of them left a lengthy epilogue of bad behavior that continued for about twenty years beyond that summer.

Part I

MIKE DONNELLY'S STORY
1883-1923

1

The Early Good Years

THE OLDER MEMBER OF THIS OUTLAW TEAM was born near Harrisburg, Pennsylvania, on April 3, 1883. He was the second of eight children of Douglas and Olivia McDonnelley. His given name at birth was Michael McDonnelley.

The family lived on their own forty-acre farm, but most of the family income came from Douglas's work as a coal miner and steel worker. Olivia stayed at home with the children—four boys and four girls. It was a fairly happy home, and Mike got along well with his brothers and sisters. The family attended the Baptist church, and the parents were strict disciplinarians. Mike resented being made to go to church as he got older and rebelled a little, but on the whole, he did not get into much trouble as a youth. He attended school regularly and was a decent student.

Douglas died when Mike was young, and Mike dropped out of school after completing the eighth grade. At age thirteen he went to work as a farm laborer. Going from farm to farm, he gradually worked his way to the cotton fields in the South. His widowed mother and the younger children continued to live on the farm near Harrisburg.

When Mike was old enough, he went to work in a fertilizer factory in Maryland. Later he returned to Pennsylvania to live with his mother and to work in the steel mills near their home. He grew up to be a tall, brawny man, reaching a height of six feet two inches and weighing over two hundred pounds.

In 1905, at age 23, Mike left his mother in Pennsylvania and headed west. During that first winter of 1905-1906, he found work as a logger in the hardwood forests of Ohio and Michigan. In early summer, he continued west, traveling all the way across the United States. In July 1906 he arrived in southwestern Washington, just in time for the wheat harvest. He went to work for a farmer named Henry Luckenbill and his wife, Stella. The Luckenbill wheat ranch was on Eureka Flats near the Touchet River, about eighteen miles northwest of Walla Walla.

After finishing the harvest on the Luckenbill ranch, Mike followed the grain harvest to the "Big Bend" country of the Columbia River Basin. There he worked for James and Bertha McDowell. The McDowell farm was in Lincoln County near the tiny community of Sassin, about three miles south of Edwall. The nearest town of any size was Cheney, about nineteen miles due east.

After the harvest was completed, Mike continued west over the Cascade Mountains to the evergreen forests of northwestern Washington. There he found employment in the logging industry again. He lived in Concrete, a town of about fifteen hundred people on the Skagit and Baker Rivers at the western edge of the Cascades.

Mike was a hardworking logger and learned the skills of his vocation well. He loved being in the forest. When he was not working as a lumberjack, he enjoyed being out in the hills, prospecting for gold.

During the years that he lived in the Skagit River Valley, Mike's behavior was no worse and no better than the average unmarried logger. He drank moderately, at least by local standards. He was a good-natured man, but he was not one to shy away from a good fight. Up and down the valley, from Sedro-Woolley to Rockport and Marblemount, this big man soon earned the reputation of being one of the strongest men around.

Mike never got into any real trouble in those days. Authorities questioned him from time to time about robberies in the area, not because they had any evidence that he was involved in any of the crimes, but merely fishing for leads. In every case Mike had an airtight alibi which eliminated him from being a suspect.

During this period, Mike McDonnelley changed his name. Fellow workers and other acquaintances continually called him Mike

McDonnell or Mike McDonald by mistake. He did not like those names, so he started using the name "Donnelly" instead of "Mc-Donnelley."

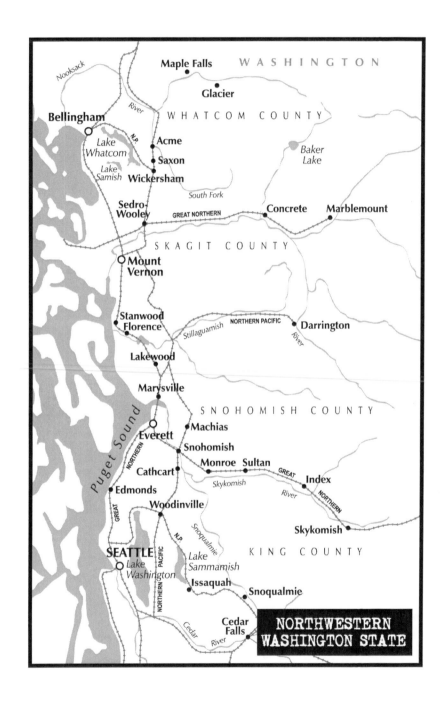

Maple Falls
Glacier
WASHINGTON
Nooksack
River
Bellingham
WHATCOM COUNTY
Lake Whatcom
N.P.
Acme
Saxon
Lake Samish
Wickersham
Baker Lake
South Fork
Sedro-Wooley
GREAT NORTHERN
Concrete
Marblemount
SKAGIT COUNTY
Mount Vernon
Stanwood
Florence
Stillaguamish
NORTHERN PACIFIC
Darrington
River
Lakewood
Marysville
SNOHOMISH COUNTY
Everett
Machias
Snohomish
Monroe
Sultan
GREAT
Index
Cathcart
Skykomish
River
NORTHERN
Edmonds
Woodinville
Snoqualmie
Skykomish
SEATTLE
Lake Washington
N.P.
NORTHERN
PACIFIC
Lake Sammamish
KING COUNTY
Issaquah
Snoqualmie
GREAT
Puget Sound
Cedar
Cedar Falls
River

NORTHWESTERN WASHINGTON STATE

2

A Good Logger Turns Outlaw

IN THE SPRING OF 1909, Mike Donnelly left Concrete and went to work cutting cedar shingle bolts not far from Bellingham, Washington. He stayed in a logging camp near Lake Samish, southwest of Lake Whatcom. At this camp he met a sixteen-year-old lad named Fred Spurgeon. (A youth of sixteen was considered old enough to do a man's work in those days.) This acquaintance would be of little importance except for the fact that these two were destined to cross paths again in the future.

In the fall of 1909, the job at Lake Samish ended. Donnelly boarded a Great Northern passenger train and rode seventy-five miles to Sultan, Washington, a town of about eight hundred fifty people in Snohomish County, situated at the confluence of the Sultan and Skykomish Rivers. The little logging community of Sultan was starting to boom, and jobs were plentiful.

Since Donnelly was a very good lumberjack and a hard worker, he easily found employment. His strength was admired by all the men who worked with him. And because he was a friendly person, he was usually befriended as well as respected by his fellow loggers. He also got along well with the townspeople of Sultan.

On July 4, 1910, as part of Sultan's Independence Day celebration, logging competitions were held. Donnelly entered and won the log-bucking contest. The winner had to saw through a big log with a crosscut saw in the fastest time. After competing in this event, most other contestants were exhausted. Some even collapsed. But Donnelly did not appear at all tired when he finished competing.

Immediately after accepting his fifty-dollar prize in Sultan that morning, he traveled eight miles west to Monroe, which was also celebrating the Fourth of July with logging competitions. Because the log-bucking contest had been delayed in starting, Donnelly arrived in time to compete in Monroe's contest as well as Sultan's. Competing in two such demanding contests in one day was unheard of.

Nearly three thousand spectators watched the popular bucking contest in Monroe that day. The log to be sawed was a big Douglas fir. The judges carefully measured and dressed down the log so that the cut made by each of the eleven contestants was exactly five feet six inches in circumference. Donnelly had to use a borrowed crosscut saw. His own saw, which was filed just the way he liked it, had been left behind in Sultan.

When the word was given to start, the sawyers attacked the log. The rhythmic, whining sound of each man's "misery whip" filled the air. Donnelly finished his cut in less than seven minutes, but this was only the fifth fastest time, which was "out of the money." In spite of not finishing first, to merely compete and do well in this strenuous logging event twice within a few hours was an amazing feat. Big Mike Donnelly was truly the "bull of the woods," in terms of strength and stamina.

In the fall of 1910, Donnelly and a friend, Bob McEvers, got jobs doing some gypo logging for Louis G. Peterson, owner of a small logging operation in Sultan. Peterson had a contract to cut cedar timber on two forty-acre tracts of land for the Trout Lake Lumber Company. He made a deal with Donnelly and McEvers to do the work. The two men had been working for a while and had $292 coming from Peterson when one day, a timber cruiser from the huge Weyerhaeuser Company came to inspect the area. The man served the gypo loggers with an injunction from the court, ordering them to stop cutting and claiming that the trees belonged to Weyerhaeuser. It was alleged that when the Trout Lake Lumber Company purchased the land from Weyerhaeuser, they did not get the rights to the timber. Weyerhaeuser claimed to have retained the timber rights.

The Weyerhaeuser Company took the financially troubled

Trout Lake Lumber Company to court. The Trout Lake Company mill, located about two miles from Sultan, was shut down, and twenty men were laid off without receiving the pay that they were owed. When Donnelly went to collect his pay, Peterson explained that since the Trout Lake Company had not yet paid him for the cedar logs that had already been delivered to the mill, he therefore did not have any money to pay Donnelly and McEvers.

The only thing that the two men could do was to file a lien on the Trout Lake Lumber Company's property for the amount of money owed. The partners then transferred the lien to a merchant in Sultan, who accepted it as payment for food, clothing, and other supplies that Donnelly and McEvers had purchased on credit before the job went bad.

While Donnelly now did not owe any money to creditors, as winter approached, he was low on cash and out of a job. No work was available. The sawmills in the area were shutting down for the winter and men were being laid off. Donnelly became very angry about the perceived injustice that he was suffering and was not shy about voicing his displeasure around town.

He was not completely broke, however. On Friday night, December 23, 1910, at the beginning of the Christmas weekend, he went to the White Front Saloon on the southwest corner of the intersection of Main and Third Streets in Sultan. There he proceeded to "celebrate" Christmas by grumbling about his situation. The more he drank, the angrier he became, until finally he started causing trouble. He got so drunk that he didn't know what was going on around him and didn't see the blow coming—a crack over the head from behind, delivered by one of his drinking companions.

Early Saturday morning, the day before Christmas, Donnelly woke up in a ditch with a cut on the top of his aching head. A quick check of his pockets revealed that all of his money had been stolen. He was now penniless as well as jobless, and revenge was on his mind. He resolved to go back to the saloon where he was robbed and get his money back.

Donnelly tried to hide his identity. He cut eyeholes in a hand-

The White Front Saloon in Sultan, Washington.
(Monroe Historical Society)

kerchief and put it across his face. Then he pulled his black slouch hat far down over his head. He was wearing his "tin pants" (water-proof pants) and a blue wool shirt—common dress for any logger.

It was about six o'clock in the morning. R. L. Jessup, one of the owners of the White Front Saloon, had just opened for business when Donnelly burst through the front door, brandishing a big .44-caliber six-shooter. There were already a half dozen laid-off loggers in the bar, drinking and visiting with Jessup. In the past, Donnelly had worked with some of these men. From Donnelly's size and the hair that was showing from under his hat, the loggers immediately recognized the holdup man.

Donnelly pointed the big revolver in a sweeping motion at the crowd, then aimed it directly at Jessup. He ordered the saloon-keeper to step out from behind the bar. Then he bunched all of the men into one corner of the saloon and went behind the bar himself. He opened the cash register and took all of the money from the till. He casually searched around among the glasses and bottles for any more money that might be hidden there, swinging his gun toward the huddled group of men from time to time to keep them at bay.

Satisfied that he'd gotten all of the saloon's money, Donnelly calmly turned his back on the crowd and walked out the door with a little less than one hundred dollars in cash.

A block away, Donnelly met up with Henry McDuff, co-owner of the White Front Saloon, who was just coming to work. Donnelly slung the revolver into McDuff's face and ordered him to stand still while he rummaged through the man's coat and pants pockets. Finding nothing of value, Donnelly turned and walked away. McDuff was relieved to get out of the situation unharmed. He had been afraid that the robber might shoot him in anger over the fact that he was not carrying any money.

Thus began Mike Donnelly's rebellion against what he perceived to be an unjust world. He was now a hardworking logger turned outlaw.

3

Shoot-out in Snohomish

THAT SAME DAY, A SHORT TIME AFTER the saloon robbery, Donnelly climbed aboard a westbound Great Northern freight train and soon was fourteen miles down the rails at Snohomish, a town of about six thousand. Donnelly did nothing to hide his identity, and as he stepped down from the freight train, a brakeman greeted him by name. Since it was the Christmas weekend, there were a thousand or two additional loggers and shingle weavers in town to celebrate the holiday. Among the revelers were some of Donnelly's friends and acquaintances. He had money again, and he was ready to celebrate Christmas with his fellow loggers.

He stopped at a restaurant and ordered a noon meal. After eating, he went to the California Wine House, on the south side of First Street between Avenue "A" and Union Avenue. The establishment had a shooting gallery and provided its customers with .22-caliber rifles with which to shoot at metal targets. Donnelly picked up one of the rifles to do some target practice.

Meanwhile, law enforcement agencies in all of Snohomish County had learned of the saloon robbery in Sultan. The police knew who they were looking for. Officers countywide were told to be on the lookout for big Mike Donnelly, and Deputy Sheriff Joseph Dunevant was sent to look for him in Snohomish.

Deputy Dunevant teamed up with the Snohomish town marshal, young Roy Norton. The two were patrolling the streets of Snohomish when, at about three p.m., they spotted Donnelly in the shooting gallery. Officer Norton was dressed in a blue policeman's uniform with a big, shiny star on his chest and a tall, domed policeman's helmet in the style of the English "bobby." If he had

First Street Looking East from Corner of Avenue "A" in Downtown Snohomish, Washington. California Wine House and Sydman's Hardware Store in foreground on right. (Snohomish Historical Society)

approached the door to the shooting gallery first, Donnelly would likely have noticed his approach and had time to react. Deputy Dunevant, however, was in plain clothes and could more likely approach the suspect without being recognized as a lawman.

Dunevant went up to the door of the California Wine House and called for Donnelly to step outside. Norton stood to one side, just outside the entrance to the shooting gallery. Donnelly set down his target rifle and came to the doorway. When Dunevant started questioning him, the suspect spotted the uniformed police officer hiding outside the door and realized that he was about to be arrested for the saloon robbery. He went for one of the two .44-caliber pistols that he had concealed in his coat pockets. Norton saw the movement of Donnelly's hand and reached to remove his own sidearm from its holster, but Donnelly beat the marshal to the draw and fired first. The bullet from Donnelly's pistol struck Norton's handcuffs, which were hanging on the left side of his belt, and was deflected. The lead slug then tore through Norton's clothing, cutting and burning a crease in the skin across his abdomen. The spent bullet then went through the lining of his heavy policeman's coat and dropped into his right coat pocket.

Norton fell down as he flinched back from the sting of the bullet, but then he quickly jumped to his feet with his service weapon drawn. He squeezed off two quick rounds in Donnelly's direction at point-blank range before Donnelly fired back again. None of these three bullets found their marks, and the gun duel ended when Donnelly pulled back into the shooting gallery and ducked behind a counter.

Officer Norton's automatic pistol jammed after his second shot. There was confusion as the loggers inside the very crowded shooting gallery realized that they were in the line of fire and scrambled to get out of the way. Most of the shooting gallery patrons crashed out through the rear window of the California Wine House. The rest of the men inside the establishment headed for the front door. Donnelly hesitated only a moment before he also bolted out the front door, using the mob of people as a shield.

Donnelly ran across First Street and a short distance west until he could get around the corner. He fled north up a long hill on Avenue "A." The two lawmen gave chase. Deputy Dunevant fired at Donnelly when he was about a half block away. Donnelly turned and responded with another shot aimed at Officer Norton, who ducked behind a pole. The marshal fired another shot in Donnelly's direction. Again all of these shots missed their marks.

The streets were fairly crowded with Christmas shoppers, and the shooting sent these citizens scurrying for cover in every direction. It was a serious situation, but not without some comic relief. When the bullets started flying, two heavy-set lumber tycoons, Tom Williams and Iver Iverson, trying to avoid being hit by a stray bullet, dove behind the same electric light pole from opposite directions. These two portly gentlemen collided behind the slender pole with a thud, knocking each other to the ground.

In a very short time a large number of private citizens—men and boys carrying rifles and shotguns—joined in the chase. After running four blocks uphill, Donnelly turned east on Fifth Street and slipped through a gap in a picket fence. He took off running to the northeast across Cecil and Clara Ferguson's field, followed by a pack of howling dogs. The mob stopped at the edge of the open field and fired at least twenty shots at long range toward Donnelly before he made it into the underbrush on the other side of the field. The fugitive was not hit. He ran headlong into the steep, swampy gulch that carried water out of Blackman's Lake to the Snohomish River. The gulch was thirty-two feet deep. At the bottom, Donnelly had to wade through ankle-deep water and mud to make his escape into the brush and trees.

Men spread out on the edge of the ravine, but no one wanted to follow Donnelly into the brush and get within range of his two revolvers. The outlaw had demonstrated that he would not hesitate to shoot to kill, and people saw him stop to reload his revolvers before he disappeared from sight in the gulch. It was also known that he purchased a large quantity of ammunition while in Snohomish and was carrying that ammunition with him.

Late Saturday afternoon, after being informed of the gunfight, Snohomish County Sheriff George B. Deering and his chief deputy, J. H. Smith, along with some other deputies, bloodhounds, and several citizens, boarded an interurban electric railway car in Everett, Washington. Everett was the county seat, situated about ten miles northwest of Snohomish. This group of lawmen headed to the Snohomish gulch to help the officers who were already at the scene.

Annoyingly, the electric streetcar derailed about three miles west of Snohomish. The sheriff and his crew and pack of dogs had to jump off the derailed car and briskly walk down the tracks the remainder of the way to town, reaching their destination after dark.

Once they were organized, the citizen posse led by Sheriff Deering surrounded the area in the gulch where Donnelly was believed to be hiding. All of the officials were armed with rifles. Some of them were expert marksmen who could pick a man off at a distance of several hundred yards.

The hounds were taken into the marsh, but they could not

pick up Donnelly's tracks. They were then taken to the place where Donnelly had entered Ferguson's field, but so many other people had been walking around the area that the dogs could not find Donnelly's trail there, either.

It was believed that Donnelly was heading toward Blackman's Lake, a shallow, swampy lake about a half-mile north of downtown Snohomish. The small lake served as a millpond for the Blackman Brothers sawmill. There was little chance that the fugitive could get out of the brushy gulch without being seen, but it was assumed that he would make a break for freedom before morning. All involved expected that any attempt to capture Donnelly would result in a fierce battle and that he would not allow himself to be taken alive.

Even though the area where Donnelly was hiding was surrounded and no one thought that he could break through the cordon of posse men, Sheriff Deering wanted to take some precautions, just in case Donnelly did manage to escape from the gulch by way of Blackman's Lake. The sheriff walked north up the road toward Machias, going door-to-door and warning residents to watch for an armed and dangerous man of Donnelly's description. Meanwhile, Deputy Sheriff Dunevant and former Snohomish police officer H.M. Evans drove to Machias to alert the authorities and advise them to be on the lookout for the fugitive.

Donnelly was very much at home in the woods and could find his way around in the dark. Using his skills, he managed to slip by the guards on the east side of the gulch. He ran a couple of blocks east to the Northern Pacific tracks, then turned south, back the way he had come, instead of going north toward Blackman's Lake as expected. It was later reported that someone was seen fleeing down the Northern Pacific Railroad tracks through the town, but by the time that the authorities received that report, Donnelly had crossed the trestle over the Snohomish River and disappeared. The report that he had escaped in that direction could not be confirmed, so lawmen continued their vigil at the gulch.

4

Running from the Law

DONNELLY, WHO AT TWENTY-EIGHT YEARS old was in excellent physical condition from a life of hard work in the woods, continued running in a southerly direction. The night was cloudy and the temperature was in the low forties. After about four and a half miles, he passed through the rural community of Cathcart, a flag stop on the Northern Pacific. He managed to catch a southbound freight train which put him into Woodinville, a little town of about three hundred residents in King County. By eight p.m. he was thirteen miles away from Snohomish.

Donnelly had gotten off the train and was walking through Woodinville when, right in the middle of town, he allegedly crossed paths with a man named Anderson. Even though it was Christmas Eve, Donnelly showed none of the Christmas spirit. He put a gun to the stranger's head and robbed him of ten dollars, which was all the money that Anderson had. The robbery victim called for the police, and Deputy Sheriff Elliott and Town Marshal Hitsman arrived within minutes. But Donnelly ran off and could not be found. From Anderson's description of the robber, there was little doubt that it was Mike Donnelly.

Reports were later received that Donnelly was seen in Everett at about ten thirty p.m. Christmas Eve by a man who said that he knew him. This man and his friend said that they saw Donnelly casually purchasing a pair of shoes and a few items of clothing at The Toggery, a men's furnishings store. The two men making the report must have been mistaken about Donnelly's identity, for the behavior of the man seen in the clothing store was not at all what one would expect from a fugitive who had been involved in a shoot-out with the police only a few hours earlier—a man who would be easily identified if seen in public. Besides, the timing of the alleged sighting in Everett did not fit with other pieces in the story.

In Woodinville the Northern Pacific Railroad intersected the old Pacific, Northshore & Eastern Railway, which had been absorbed by the Northern Pacific as one of its branch lines. Donnelly caught a freight train on this branch line, which took him around the north end of Lake Washington and into Ballard, a part of Seattle where he could easily blend in with the fishermen, seamen, and other loggers who hung out there. He had money left from the Sultan saloon robbery, plus the ten dollars from the holdup in Woodinville, so he could afford a room in Seattle in which to lie low for a few days.

On Sunday—Christmas morning—the manhunt resumed in and around Snohomish, but Donnelly could not be found. The search was finally called off. The outlaw made good his escape, much to the embarrassment of the Snohomish County sheriff's office.

5

A Partner in Crime

AFTER A FEW DAYS IN SEATTLE, Donnelly made his way to Black River Junction, a station on the south side of Seattle where the Northern Pacific intersected the Columbia & Puget Sound Railroad. There he teamed up with a man known as "Slim," whose complete identity has never been learned. Slim was a tall man, only an inch shorter and a little older than Donnelly, but much thinner. He was apparently someone Donnelly had known when he lived in Concrete. The two men decided to leave Black River Junction and go back to Concrete together.

On their way north the pair got off the train near Stanwood to visit Donnelly's former logging partner, Bob McEvers, who lived in a shack on the beach south of Stanwood. McEvers was glad to see his old friend from Sultan and invited the men to stay the night and celebrate New Year's Eve with him. The next morning, after seeing in the New Year with their friend, Donnelly and Slim caught a northbound Northern Pacific train to Sedro-Woolley. From there they caught an eastbound Great Northern freight train and arrived in Concrete late in the evening of January 1, 1911.

Early Monday morning, January 2, Donnelly and Slim walked up to the Eagle Bar inside the Superior Hotel in Concrete. They pointed revolvers at the owner, Joseph Janisch, and the bartender. The robbers told the saloonkeepers to put their hands in the air and not move. They then helped themselves to the New Year's weekend receipts. They were turning to leave with the cash when trigger-happy Donnelly needlessly opened fire and shot up the saloon, breaking bottles and drinking glasses and causing Janisch and the bartender to dive for cover on the floor behind the bar.

Donnelly and Slim returned to their hideout in Concrete and spent the rest of the day putting together packs and bedrolls, preparing to survive the harsh winter conditions they would face while on the run in the forests of northwestern Washington. On Tuesday, January 3, the pair of desperadoes headed west from Concrete for about four miles and then turned north. They crossed Grandby Creek and hiked up the steep divide between the Skagit River Valley and the South Fork of the Nooksack River in Whatcom County. It was three or four hard miles to the top of the divide. Donnelly and Slim were familiar with the trails. From the top of the ridge, they had two miles of steep trail down to the river. They camped that night in the wilds on the South Fork of the Nooksack, eleven or twelve miles from Concrete. It was cloudy and cold, in the high thirties, but at least it was not raining.

In the morning they continued downstream on the South Fork of the Nooksack, and on Wednesday afternoon they showed up at the Key City Logging Company camp (formerly the Ferguson Logging camp) near the Saxon Bridge. The logging camp was owned by E. A. Sims and Everett B. Deming of Bellingham. The fugitives were now about twenty cross-country miles from Concrete.

At the logging camp they asked the camp foreman, Winslow B. Stevens, Jr., for a job, thinking that a remote logging camp would be a perfect place for them to hide from the police for the rest of the winter. Informed that the camp was not hiring, the men then asked if they could spend the night in the bunkhouse. Not wanting to be unkind, Stevens granted them permission to sleep there that night.

The next morning, after the logging crew went to work, Donnelly and Slim ate breakfast at the cookhouse. When the cook tried to collect payment for the breakfast, the men said that they were broke and could not pay. Concerned that these penniless "hoboes" might try to steal food or something, the cook and the bull cook, Sigard Ousdal, told the men to hit the road immediately after breakfast and not to remain hanging around the camp.

The two men left the logging camp and continued in a northwesterly direction, walking about a mile down a logging railroad called Saxon Spur, which led from the Key City camp to a flag stop on the Northern Pacific called Saxon. At this point the little logging railroad merged with the main railroad line, about two miles southeast of the small community of Acme, Washington.

When the men arrived at Saxon, they found a large sealed carton sitting in the little unmanned switch house at the junction. Since there was no one around to stop them, they opened the box to see if it contained anything of value. The package turned out to be a case of new leather logging boots. Pleased with their find, the men each discarded their old shoes, put on new boots from the carton, and selected a second pair to take with them. This petty theft turned out to be a big mistake, because it later drew a great deal of unwanted attention to the outlaws.

Win Stevens, who had ordered the case of logging boots for his crew, had been notified by telephone that morning that the carton would be set off the local freight train at Saxon station, where there was no agent to look after them. Stevens telephoned Aanet Thompson, a teamster who was due to deliver vegetables, and asked him to pick up the case of boots on his way up to camp.

Thompson was driving his team of horses near the railroad when he met two men walking down the tracks toward Acme. He noticed that each man had a new pair of logging boots hanging from his bedroll. At Saxon he found the opened case of boots and figured that the men he had seen had rifled through the box. He put the remaining boots in his wagon and took them to the logging camp.

Thompson told Win Stevens about the two men he'd seen carrying new boots. He said that both men were dressed alike in black logger jeans with wide suspenders, blue flannel shirts, black coats, and slouch hats. One was tall and heavyset. The other was almost as tall but stooped over when he walked. From the description, Stevens was sure that they were the same men who had spent the previous night in his bunkhouse.

The angry camp boss telephoned storeowner Frederick "Fritz" Zobrist in Acme, a town of about three hundred people, and asked him to watch for the thieves and to detain them if he could. When Stevens described the suspects, Zobrist informed him that the pair had just left his store after buying a can of tomatoes, some crackers, and other things for lunch. With Stevens still on the phone, Zobrist looked out and watched the men stopped to eat their lunch at G. W. Miller's shingle shed beside the railroad tracks, about a hundred yards south of the general store. Zobrist told Stevens that it appeared the two men were going to stay in Acme at least long enough to eat lunch. Stevens responded that he was on his way to town.

At the time, a young man named Jimmy Ness was hanging around in Zobrist's store After his conversation with Stevens, Zobrist sent Jimmy down to the shingle shed to try to keep the two suspects from leaving.

Village of Acme in Whatcom County, Washington. A little after noon on January 5, 1911, Mike Donnelly and his partner, "Slim," purchased some things to eat at Frederick Zobrist's store [on the left] and went down the N. P. track to Miller's shingle shed [just out of the photo to the right] to eat their lunch. (Sylvia Anderson collection #1994.38.20, Whatcom Museum of History & Art)

6

Fatal Gunfight at Acme

EVEN THOUGH ACME WAS A DRY TOWN where the possession of alcohol was illegal, Jimmy Ness had a bottle of whiskey in his pocket. Inside the shingle shed he proceeded to "entertain" the two strangers. Jim began telling them his hard-luck story and offered to share his whiskey with them. Donnelly and Slim, in turn, invited Jim to help himself to the food. The robbers noticed that Jim's shoes were in pretty bad shape, and they told him about the box of boots at Saxon Spur where he could just help himself to a new pair.

A short time later, a little before three p.m., foreman Win Stevens drove into Acme. He stopped at Zobrist's store, where Fritz Zobrist pointed out the shingle shed that he had seen the suspects enter. Stevens then drove north across the river and continued a short distance upstream to the home of the justice of the peace, Judge Audley A. Galbraith, Sr., a longtime Acme resident. Stevens asked Galbraith to deputize him and then accompany him to help make the arrest.

Aud Galbraith was a peace-loving man who did not believe in carrying a gun, but he owned an old .32-caliber pistol that he loaned to Stevens, although he had only two rounds of ammunition for the revolver. Stevens and Galbraith went back to town and walked down the railroad tracks to the shingle shed. They thought that they were about to arrest two hoboes whose only crime was stealing a couple of pairs of boots.

The shed was a shingle load-out from which the Miller Shingle Company loaded their cedar product into railroad cars. On the track side of the shed, sixty-year-old Galbraith climbed up on a platform that was about five feet above the ground. From there he could look down on the men inside the shed. The suspects were sitting facing each other, about three feet apart, eating their lunch, which was laid out on a shingle "tray."

There was a doorway in the side of the shed opposite of where Galbraith was standing. Stevens walked through this doorway into the area where the suspects were sitting. He bent over and picked up a pack with a pair of new shoes hanging from it. Just then Galbraith shouted loudly from above, "Put your hands up! You are under arrest!"

The words were barely out of Galbraith's mouth when the man called Slim whipped out his revolver and started shooting. He was not about to be taken into custody for petty theft when he had more serious charges facing him. Slim's first shot hit the unarmed Galbraith above the heart and knocked him down. The second shot whizzed above the fallen man, missing him completely. At the same instant, Donnelly spun around to his left and saw Stevens, two feet away. Donnelly drew and fired a slug into Stevens' back. Slim turned and also shot at Stevens, hitting him and slightly wounding him in the leg. Jimmy Ness ran for his life, back to the store.

The two desperadoes leaped from the shed and ran down the Northern Pacific railroad tracks to the south. The seriously wounded Stevens pulled himself up, drew his borrowed revolver, and fired two quick shots at the fleeing men—the only two rounds that the pistol held. He succeeded in hitting Donnelly in the lumbar region of his left side, about belt-high.

Stevens then helped Aud Galbraith stumble back to the store. Galbraith, holding his hand to his chest, said that he thought he was badly hurt. Zobrist and Stevens laid Galbraith down on the floor and sent Jimmy Ness for help, but Justice Galbraith died the moment he lay down.

Win Stevens felt that he might be mortally wounded himself. The bullet from Donnelly's pistol had entered his back, struck a rib, and traveled around the rib cage under his back muscles, lodging in his abdomen. The wound was extremely painful. Fritz Zobrist got on the telephone and called the county sheriff's office in Bellingham.

Donnelly and Slim fled down the tracks in the direction from which they had come. The mainline track went back through Saxon to the tiny town of Wickersham on the Samish River, about five miles south of Acme. The outlaws were immediately pursued by a dozen or more employees from the Miller Shingle Company and the Anderson & Smith Shingle Company, armed with every conceivable type of firearm.

The stretch of track leading out of Acme was perfectly straight for a considerable distance. From time to time the fugitives turned and pointed their .38-caliber semi-automatic Colt pistols at the crowd of men who were chasing them, causing the pursuers to stop and take cover. Each time this happened, the fugitives got a little farther ahead of the posse. No more shots were actually fired.

The fleeing men left the tracks and ran up a skid road that led into the hills to the west, disappearing from sight around a turn. Some of the pursuers stopped and marked the spot where the men were last seen, while others spread out and took up protected positions along the tracks. It was already twilight and would be completely dark in about an hour and a half. The workers would not follow the fugitives into the woods until reinforcements arrived.

A short distance up the trail, out of sight, the fleeing gunmen left the skid road and doubled back on their pursuers. Donnelly was too badly hurt to run any farther. The men barricaded themselves behind a large log just off the side of the road and waited, ready to ambush and kill anyone who chased them up the skid trail. If any of the citizens giving chase had foolishly followed the fugitives into the woods that evening, there undoubtedly would have been bloodshed.

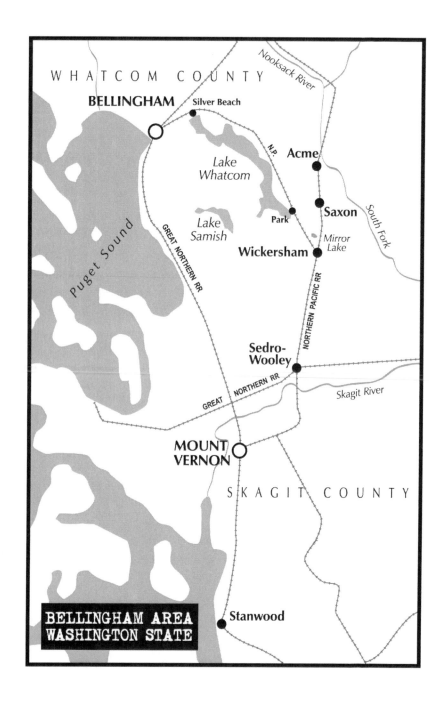

**BELLINGHAM AREA
WASHINGTON STATE**

7

Caring for the Wounded

AS SOON AS THE SHERIFF'S OFFICE in Bellingham was informed of the shootings, authorities called the Northern Pacific Railway depot in Bellingham and had the three o'clock train held at the station until several Whatcom County deputy sheriffs could board. Whatcom County Sheriff Spencer B. VanZandt, in Maple Falls, Washington, on official business, was unable to personally respond to the call from Acme.

Bellingham was twelve miles west of Acme. The Whatcom County deputies, including Sheriff Charles W. Stevenson of neighboring Skagit County, arrived on the scene of the shootings just before dark. They brought with them the Skagit County bloodhounds, "Mike" and "Brady," who were famous for finding a little lost boy in the wilds of nearby Canyon Creek the previous summer.

When the bloodhounds arrived, darkness had already fallen. The team of lawmen immediately began organizing a manhunt, but little could be done in the dark except to place guards on the roads and trails for the night. Farmers and logging-camp personnel in every direction were notified by telephone to be on the lookout for these armed and dangerous men.

Guards were dispatched north from Wickersham and assigned to guard the railroad and every road coming south out of Acme, as well as roads going north and west toward Mirror Lake, about three-quarters of a mile from Wickersham.

At eight thirty p.m., the sheriff's department chartered a large gasoline-powered launch named the *Romona*, owned by George Jenkins. Jenkins was hired to carry guards from Silver Beach, a suburb east of Bellingham at the northernmost point on Lake Whatcom, to the community of Park, about eleven miles south. More guards were recruited at Park. This combined posse covered every approach to Lake Whatcom from the Wickersham and Acme areas. All road guards had orders to stop and examine anyone who tried to pass down any of the roads or railroad tracks.

Aboard the *Romona*, Deputy Sheriff Warren Slater and another special deputy patrolled the shoreline at the upper end of Lake Whatcom throughout the night. Armed to the teeth and carrying electric flashlights, they cruised back and forth between Park and Blue Canyon to make sure that the fugitives could not escape by going over the mountains west of the place where they had last been seen.

Meanwhile, Donnelly was very sick. He was too badly wounded to travel very far, but Slim would not abandon him. After waiting in ambush until it was nearly dark, the fugitives quietly made their way back, undetected, to the railroad track near Acme. Elaborate measures were taken to keep these killers from escaping to the south or west, but no one had expected them to go the short distance north back to Acme, so that route was unguarded.

Kirk Stevens, the eighteen-year-old son of Win Stevens, was working at the Key City Company logging camp when he was called and told that his father had been shot. The elder Stevens was placed aboard the same Great Northern train that had brought lawmen to Acme from Bellingham. The train waited at Acme until Kirk Stevens arrived from camp to accompany his father to the hospital.

As the two fugitives approached the railroad tracks at Acme, they were surprised to find a train stopped and waiting. Ironically, the men who had shot Win Stevens and Aud Galbraith climbed into an empty boxcar on the same train that was taking their wounded victim to the hospital.

The train carrying both the victim and the outlaws rolled past the unsuspecting guards stationed on the tracks south of Acme and did not stop until it reached the Great Northern depot in Sedro-Woolley, a small city of forty-two hundred people in Skagit County, about twenty-three miles south of Acme. Win Stevens was taken four blocks from the depot to the Frazee General Hospital at the north end of Rita Street. The hospital was located in what had once been a residence, across from the St. Charles Hotel.

While Stevens was being transported to the hospital, Donnelly, with his partner's help, climbed down from the boxcar that had brought them to Sedro-Woolley. The outlaws made their way undetected to the Grays Harbor Lodging House, located a very short distance from the depot on the northwest corner of the intersection of Southern Avenue and Metcalf Street. Slim told the proprietor of the lodging house, Mrs. Julia Kelly, that his friend had fallen on a spike and needed a room in which to rest. The men had money from the saloon robbery in Concrete and paid cash in advance. Julia Kelly's daughter showed the men to their room. Slim stayed in the room with Donnelly through the night.

At the hospital, Dr. Charles M. Frazee examined Win Stevens' wound and decided that he did not have the necessary skills to risk removing the bullet by himself. He gave Stevens a sedative and some opiates to kill the pain and sent to Seattle for Dr. Lowe France, a more experienced surgeon, to perform the operation. Word was also sent to Stevens' home in Snohomish, about forty-six miles away. His wife of twenty-three years, Grace (Sheldon), and their other son, twenty-one-year-old Jerome Stevens, came from Snohomish to Sedro-Woolley to be with their husband and father.

Stevens was wheeled into surgery Friday morning, January 6. Dr. France, assisted by Dr. Frazee and his nurse (and wife), Gudra Frazee, removed the bullet and repaired some of the damage caused by the gunshot. Unfortunately the doctors apparently did not see that Stevens had a lacerated artery. They would not have seen the damaged artery if it were not hemorrhaging, possibly because a tamponade—an abnormal swelling of the tissue around a wound—was putting pressure on the artery, preventing it from bleeding. After removing the bullet, the surgeons announced that, while Stevens' wounds were serious, they were not life-threatening, as long as they did not become infected.

Frazee Hospital at Sedro-Woolley, Washington. On January 6, 1911, Win Stevens, Jr., underwent surgery at this hospital for a gunshot wound inflicted by Mike Donnelly. Stevens died later that day. (Skagit River Journal of History)

8

An Empty Search for Fugitives

THE DAY AFTER THE SHOOTINGS, Whatcom County Sheriff Spencer B. VanZandt and Deputy Sheriff Wallace Coleman, both stranded at Maple Falls the night before, came down to Acme to lead the manhunt for the murderers. A large number of volunteers had joined the posse through the night. At daybreak on the same morning that Win Stevens, Jr., went into surgery, the dogs, "Mike" and "Brady," and the large posse started up the skid road where the fugitives were last seen. The old shoes that Donnelly and Slim had thrown away when they put on the stolen boots were used to give the bloodhounds the scent.

The posse found where the two men had lain in ambush. Donnelly's wound did not have much external bleeding, so the searchers found no blood and did not know that one of the outlaws was wounded. The dogs were very interested in sniffing the area where the fugitives had been and did not want to leave that spot. But the dog handlers became impatient, pulled the dogs off of that scent, and started them up the skid trail. However, the dogs were not immediately able to track the suspects back to Acme, because Donnelly had scattered fine red pepper powder to cover their tracks. He always carried a bag of red pepper in his pocket expressly for that purpose, just in case the need ever arose. He knew that the pepper would burn the hounds' noses and make it impossible for them to pick up a scent.

Soon the hounds were on the trail of something else. No one knows what scent they were following, but the posse at the time assumed that they were on the trail of the fugitives. This new trail led up the old skid road a short distance and then into some fallen timber and debris from earlier logging operations. It was very difficult for the men to stumble through the brush and debris where the dogs were leading. The posse should have known that it was not likely that the fugitives would choose a route where the going was so hard and slow, but no one doubted the experienced dogs.

For hours these well-trained bloodhounds slowly and carefully worked over the trail that they were on. The large group of man-hunters following behind the dogs, confident that they were on the trail. There was no evidence that the fugitives had split up or doubled back. They were assumed to be running straight for Mirror Lake and the head of Lake Whatcom.

Shortly after noon, the hounds came to the edge of a small pond near the logging camps of the Moore Logging Company and the Herbert Dahlen Shingle Company. This pond supplied water for Dahlen's flume, which floated cedar shingle bolts down to the mill, two miles away. Near the pond the dogs lost the trail. At this point the posse was about six miles from Acme.

The surrounding country was virtually impassable, wild and broken and covered with logging debris. Not knowing that the men they were looking for had gone to Sedro-Woolley on the train the night before, the posse thought for sure that the fleeing men were trapped. There were only three possible outlets from the place where the dogs had led the posse. One possibility was that the men could have floated on the water in the flume down to Dahlen's shingle mill to the east. Two, they could have traveled on a tramway that also ran east down the mountainside. The tram was used to send logs from the logging camp to a spur on the Northern Pacific Railroad. Or, three, they could have followed a mountain trail go-ing south through the woods to Mirror Lake, from which point they could have gotten to the town of Park at the head of Lake Whatcom. Any attempt to flee north or west across the rugged and steep terrain in those directions would surely lead to death from exposure or starvation, since the January temperatures were in the low forties and raining.

The guards on the three potential escape routes were heavily reinforced. Even though no fourth escape route was considered, just to make sure, some posse men spread out through the broken and timbered country, thus completely surrounding the area. To the south and east of the search area, men were patrolling every inch of the Acme Road east of the logging camps, waiting for the outlaws to come that way. They were spread out along the railroad all the way from the end of the log tramway at Dahlen's Spur to Wickersham and back up to Park. It was thought that the hunted men were bottled up and escape was impossible. The posse prepared themselves for a bloody battle when the time finally came to attempt to capture the desperate fugitives.

After the dogs were given a well-deserved rest, they began searching around and around the pond near the logging camp. The hounds went in wider and wider circles out from the spot where they lost the trail, but they did not pick up a scent. The posse continued to search for a couple of hours, but when the bloodhounds failed to find a trail leading away from the flume pond, it was decided that the wanted men must have jumped into the flume and ridden the water chute down the mountainside. That was the only logical explanation for the dogs' inability to smell them.

At about three p.m., the posse and the dogs shifted the focus of their search from the mountain to the valley at the foot of the flume, about two miles north of Wickersham. It was speculated that the men might have gone into the hills near Wickersham in an attempt to get back into the Skagit River Valley, where they were from. The bloodhounds were driven around the area in an open horse-drawn buggy to see if they could detect the scent of the fugitives in the air. The hounds did a lot of loud, mournful baying, but smelled nothing. It was completely dark at a few minutes after five p.m., and the search was called off.

9

Second Victim Dies

EARLY FRIDAY MORNING, Slim left his partner in bed in their room at the Grays Harbor Lodging House. He knew that Donnelly's prognosis was not good, and while he was worried about his friend, he could not stay and risk being caught himself. Slim took Donnelly's pistols and hid them in a vent in the hallway outside the room, thinking that it would be better if his partner were unarmed if captured. Slim paid another night's rent on the room, left the lodging house, and slipped away, making a run for his own life.

He hiked five miles southwest to the town of Burlington. There he caught a Northern Pacific freight train for a sixteen-mile ride to Stanwood. He reached the home of Bob McEvers near Stanwood by noon on Friday. Slim told McEvers about Donnelly's serious problem and pleaded with McEvers to go to Sedro-Woolley to check on Donnelly and get medical help for him. Slim drew a map of the location of Donnelly's room in the Grays Harbor Lodging House and gave it to McEvers. He then left, and no one ever heard from him again.

McEvers asked another logger friend to go with him, and the two were in Sedro-Woolley that evening. But they went to the wrong building. Instead of going to the Grays Harbor Lodging House, they mistakenly went to the Vendome Hotel on the southeast corner of the intersection of Ferry Street and Eastern Avenue, not far from the Frazee Hospital. Of course they could not find Mike Donnelly, because he was not there. As they were going room to room in the hotel looking for Donnelly, the two loggers aroused the suspicion of the hotel management. When confronted, they made up an excuse for being there and left without getting help for the wounded man.

Earlier on Friday afternoon, when the swelling had gone down, Win Stevens started bleeding internally from the lacerated artery that the doctors had missed. He underwent emergency surgery, but the hemorrhaging could not be stopped, and he bled to death at about nine p.m. on Friday evening, January 6, 1911. His wife and his sons, Jerome and Kirk, were at his side.

10

"Slim" Gets Away

THE ROOMING HOUSE PROPRIETRESS, Julia Kelly, became increasingly uneasy about her injured tenant, whom she had observed looked very weak when he checked in and whom she had not seen since that time. When the wounded man's partner came down in the morning and told Julia that his friend was still not feeling well and would be staying in bed for awhile, she thought it strange that Slim paid another day's rent, then left and never returned.

Late Friday evening, Mrs. Kelly telephoned the deputy town marshal, Jasper "Jap" Holman, and asked him to come over. She took Marshal Holman to Donnelly's room and he forced the door open. There they found Donnelly near death from the loss of blood. Holman knew instantly that this man was one of the subjects of a massive manhunt in the area. The wounded suspect was placed under arrest and immediately taken to St. Elizabeth Hospital on the southwest corner of Township Street and Fildalgo Street in Sedro-Woolley. After one look at Donnelly, the doctors said that they did not expect him to live.

Donnelly underwent surgery on Saturday to save him from almost certain death. The internal bleeding had stopped, but blood had collected in his abdominal cavity. Surgeon W. A. Dorsey drew some of the blood off and did some exploratory procedures, but Donnelly was not opened up and the bullet was not removed. The patient was very weak, and the doctor felt that there was no way that he could survive, saying that if he had undergone surgery sooner, perhaps he could have been saved. Now they would just have to let nature take its course.

St. Elizabeth Hospital in Sedro-Woolley, Washington. Murder suspect Mike Donnelly was arrested on the evening of January 6, 1911, and taken to this hospital for treatment of a serious gunshot wound. (Skagit River Journal of History)

After learning from the lodging house proprietor that another man known only as "Slim"—probably the murderer of Audley Galbraith—had been in Sedro-Woolley with Donnelly on Friday, the police engaged in an intensive manhunt. They had no reliable clue to his identity, but if they did apprehend the right man, Julia Kelly and her daughter would be able to identify him. The police were also looking for Jimmy Ness, who had talked with Donnelly and Slim in the shingle shed in Acme. They felt that Ness could help with the identification of Aud Galbraith's murderer, when and if the right suspect was captured.

Some lawmen thought that the killer still at large was Jim Hill of Maple Falls, Washington, who was already wanted for murdering a man named Sam Thompson. Hill had disappeared after the Maple Falls murder, three weeks earlier. It was believed that Slim's behavior in the Acme shingle shed indicated that he was a desperate man who had a lot to lose if captured. Joseph Janisch's description of the shorter man who had robbed his saloon, and Win Stevens' description of the shorter man who had stayed at the Key City Logging camp, fit Jim Hill's description exactly. But even if Jim Hill was the man whom they wanted, no one had any idea where to look for him.

Law enforcement officers throughout the area were on the lookout for any possible suspect. All suspicious-looking characters and strangers were stopped and questioned. On Friday night, January 6, a deputy sheriff tried to detain a man at Wickersham, but the man resisted. The deputy shot and killed the poor man. Witnesses said that the dead man was not Slim. He was later identified as L. K. Hymans of Seattle.

On Saturday morning, Bob McEvers made an anonymous telephone call to a doctor in Sedro-Woolley and told him about a wounded fugitive lying in a rooming house somewhere in town. McEvers did not know that Donnelly was already in custody and hoped that his call would result in getting help for his former logging partner.

Authorities were notified of the anonymous call, and a sweep was made of the area in an attempt to find the caller. They picked up Bob McEvers near Sedro-Woolley, not knowing that he had any connection to the killer, but simply because he was a stranger to them and they wanted to find out who he was and what he was doing there. When they found a sketch of the Grays Harbor Lodging House in his possession, the police thought that they may have picked up Slim, but witnesses told them that McEvers was not Donnelly's partner.

McEvers told authorities a story about meeting a man on the road while walking up from Burlington. He said the man had given him the map and some money and had asked him to check on his sick friend at the rooming house. McEvers said that he had no idea who the stranger was. The police accepted McEvers' story for the time being and he was released.

On Sunday evening, January 8, the police in Everett received a call that a suspicious-looking man had been spotted coming out of the brush and going into the Cadillac Hotel in Machias, north of Snohomish. Deputy Sheriff R. Markham and Detectives John Sturgus and Basil Wells of the Everett city police drove a rig to Machias and arrested the man, despite the fact that he was about fifty years old and quite gray and only slightly fit the description of the man called Slim. The man was Austrian and said that his name was Tom Chelolio. He was unarmed and offered no resistance. When Deputy Sheriff Robert Cruikshank of Bellingham took Chelolio to the Grays Harbor Lodging House in Sedro-Woolley, the owners there were positive that he was not the man who had brought Donnelly to their place.

Another man was seen prowling through the woods near Lyman, in Skagit County, on Wednesday, January 11. A posse and bloodhounds went looking for him for questioning. The man appeared to be desperate to escape capture and got away by cutting the cable on a Skagit River ferry after crossing the river. The suspect also cut several telephone lines in areas that he passed through. It was thought that this might be Donnelly's pal Slim—whoever Slim was—but the man got away.

On Wednesday, January 18, a police officer spotted a man named William Davidson on a Seattle street. Davidson had formerly worked in a livery stable in Concrete. The officer thought the man might be Donnelly's partner and called for backup. Seattle lawmen moved in to make an arrest. Davidson ran when he saw the officers coming, but was captured after a short chase. It was later determined that he was not the murderer of Aud Galbraith.

Also on January 18, police visited Bob McEvers at his home near Stanwood. They suspected that he knew more about Slim than he was telling and wanted to question him for a second time. In fact, they suspected that on January 7, after McEvers was released from police custody the first time, he teamed up with the outlaw Slim and together they "stole some stuff" at the site of a new bridge being built near Sedro-Woolley. The thieves, whoever they were, later abandoned the stolen goods at Fir, about thirteen miles southwest of Sedro-Woolley and less than ten miles from where Bob

McEvers lived.

McEvers denied that he had anything to do with the theft of bridge-building materials and denied knowing anything more about the fugitive they were seeking than what he had already told the police. The investigators had no justifiable reason to detain McEvers or question him further, so they released him. He would not play any future role in their case.

On Friday, January 20, Sheriff Louis A. Thomas of Whatcom County brought a man named McDonald to the Grays Harbor Lodging House in Sedro-Woolley. McDonald had been arrested in West Minster because he "resembled in some respects" the fugitive Slim. When Mrs. Kelly confirmed that McDonald was not Slim, Sheriff Thomas gave the man some money for his trouble and told him that he was free to go.

On Wednesday, January 25, Deputy Sheriff Wilson Stewart of Whatcom County brought a gentleman named Claude Pulsifer to Sedro-Woolley. Pulsifer had been arrested in the little town of Brinnon in Jefferson County, on the west side of Hood Canal, for the "crime" of looking like Slim. Again, witnesses said that the police had the wrong man.

The manhunt continued, with more men being detained on suspicion only. These false reports of Slim's supposed capture continued to appear so often in newspapers that the phrase "Where's Slim?" became a joke in the media.

Rewards totaling $1,750 were offered for information leading to the arrest of the mysterious murderer of Aud Galbraith. On Saturday afternoon, January 14, Whatcom County commissioners approved a reward of $500 for the capture of Slim. To sweeten the pot, the State of Washington offered a reward of $250. The Galbraith family offered a reward of $500, and E. A. Sims, manager and part owner of the Key City Logging Company offered a reward of $500. All of the reward offers were official and registered with the auditor of Whatcom County.

Mike Donnelly refused to disclose "Slim's" real name and, in fact, gave false information about his partner to throw investigators off. He seemed to take pride in helping his partner escape. With no other clue to his identity than his general appearance, finding the murderer would be almost impossible unless someone who knew him gave him up for the reward.

Although authorities throughout the Pacific Northwest conducted an intensive investigation, they turned up no new leads. The murderer of Audley A. Galbraith, Sr., was never apprehended, nor was his true identity ever learned.

11

Wounded Prisoner Survives

IN THE MEANTIME, MIKE DONNELLY was making a steady recovery. The internal bleeding had stopped. Sheriff George Deering checked on the condition of his prisoner at St. Elizabeth Hospital on Sunday, January 8, two days after the suspect was arrested and taken to the hospital, and was told that Donnelly's condition had improved somewhat, but his chances of surviving were still only one in a thousand. By Wednesday, Donnelly had improved even more and his chances of survival were growing better daily. However, he was still not out of danger of dying suddenly at any time. A nurse at the hospital said that Donnelly had expressed a desire to live and that he often inquired about his chances of recovery. On Thursday, January 12, Dr. Dorsey removed the bullet from Donnelly's right side, and his condition was upgraded to fair. The superintendent at St. Elizabeth's Hospital, J. B. Alexander, requested a twenty-four-hour police guard on Donnelly, predicting that the murder suspect would get well.

Donnelly's wound became infected because it had not been properly drained and cleaned in the beginning. On Thursday, January 19, doctors performed an operation to drain the abscessed wound. Donnelly's general good health made it possible for him to fight off the infection and he continued to improve. He remained in the hospital for two months.

Finally, after he had sufficiently recuperated from his gunshot wound to be safely moved, Donnelly was taken to the county jail in Bellingham. The jail was in the basement of the large Whatcom County courthouse on Farragut Street between "G" Street and "H" Street. Doctors said that Donnelly was still too weak to be placed in a regular jail cell with the other prisoners. A cot was set up in

Whatcom County Courthouse at Bellingham, Washington. Mike
Donnelly was taken to the jail in the basement of the Whatcom County
courthouse around the first of March, 1911, to await trial for murder in one
of the courtrooms upstairs. (Whatcom Museum of History & Art, Bellingham, Washington)

the corridor outside of the inner cellblock, where the frail prisoner
remained in bed both day and night.

The inner cellblock was where prisoners were normally locked
in separate cells for the night and where they were kept at other
times when there was a need for greater security. In the corridor
where Donnelly slept, all prisoners ate their meals, and those who
had not lost their privileges were allowed in the corridor at other
times for recreation.

Donnelly was a cooperative prisoner, friendly and talkative. He
had a droll sense of humor and joked with his captors. But this was
Donnelly's first time behind bars, and he was a man who loved being outdoors in the woods. As he began feeling better, he quickly
realized that he was not willing or able to accept being confined.
He immediately began thinking about breaking out of jail. As he
lay awake in his cot, he carefully observed the jail's routines—where

things were kept, the times people came and went, etc.—looking for weaknesses in jail security.

On Friday night, March 17, 1911, four young men were brought into the Whatcom County jail on charges of burglary. They were Harry Thomassen, Jr., age nineteen, his brother Robert Thomassen, age seventeen, Fred Spurgeon, age eighteen, and his brother Ray Spurgeon, age fifteen. This gang of youths, led by Fred Spurgeon, had broken into and robbed a half dozen stores and a school in south Bellingham during the previous few months. The previous Thursday, the youths had appeared in Judge John A. Kellogg's court with their parents, and they all eventually pleaded guilty to second-degree burglary.

In addition to the burglary charges, Fred Spurgeon pleaded guilty to assaulting a grocery clerk with a deadly weapon a few months earlier. At midnight on Christmas night, December 25, 1910, Spurgeon and his gang were breaking into the Kinsey Grocery Store at 2011 Harris Avenue in south Bellingham. Louis Hibbs, who worked as a clerk for Mr. Kinsey and lived on the corner right next door to the store, was awakened by the sound of breaking glass. He slipped his clothes on and went to the rear of the store building. In the dark, Hibbs almost bumped into the group of young men who were robbing the store. The startled burglars ran toward the street and Lou Hibbs gave chase. Before Hibbs knew what was happening, Fred Spurgeon turned and opened fire with his revolver, and Hibbs started dodging bullets. Fortunately none of the five shots fired found their marks; but for Fred Spurgeon, this was another serious offense added to the burglary charges. On the charge of assault with a deadly weapon, Spurgeon was sentenced to a maximum of fifteen years in jail.

The two minor gang members were sent to a juvenile facility at Chehalis, Washington. Fred Spurgeon and Harry Thomassen, Jr., were held as adults in the county jail while awaiting transfer to the state reformatory at Monroe, Washington. In the jail, Mike Donnelly and Fred Spurgeon got together and visited with one another whenever prisoners were allowed to socialize. The two men had worked together a year and a half earlier near Lake Samish, where they both had been shingle bolt cutters. Spurgeon was surprised to find the popular lumberjack in jail and to hear that he was charged with murder.

Throughout his criminal career, Donnelly had a way of getting others to help him with his schemes, and this was the beginning of that phenomenon. He soon convinced the cocky young Spurgeon to help him with an escape plan that he had conceived.

12

Attempted Jail Break

WHATCOM COUNTY SHERIFF LOUIS A. THOMAS sometimes hired his twenty-year-old son, Louis Athelbert Thomas, Jr., to act as jailer at the county jail. Donnelly told Spurgeon that he had noticed that young Mr. Thomas did not always strictly follow established jailhouse procedures. For example, the jailer was never armed. When the prisoners were gathered as a group in the middle corridor and then sent back to their individual cells, young Thomas did not bother to do a head check. And when Thomas entered the middle corridor where Donnelly's cot was located, he did not bother to lock the outer door behind him. Donnelly also told Spurgeon that the jailer kept an automatic pistol in an unlocked drawer in the pantry in the kitchen. He then explained his plan for a jailbreak—a plan that took advantage of these weaknesses in security.

The planned jailbreak was set into motion on the afternoon of Wednesday, March 29, when Athelbert Thomas was filling in for the regular jailer. As part of the plan, Spurgeon armed himself with a metal leg from his bunk. He concealed the makeshift weapon under his clothing, in case something in the plan went wrong. At about five p.m., after Donnelly and the twelve other prisoners had finished eating their evening meal, jailer Thomas ordered them back into the main holding tank so that he could pick up their dirty dishes and take them to the kitchen to be washed. He did not bother to check the men in their individual cells to see that they were all accounted for. Using levers in his outer office, Thomas locked the doors to the inner tank where most of the prisoners were sent. He then unlocked and entered the middle corridor where Donnelly lay in his bunk. The jailer did not lock the outer door after he entered.

Fred Spurgeon was hiding under Donnelly's cot. When young Thomas turned his back, he rolled out from under the cot and slipped out through the open jail door, locking the door behind him. He went directly to the pantry to get the automatic pistol kept there.

Thomas turned and saw what Spurgeon had done, but the young jailer was now locked behind the steel jail door himself and could do nothing. Harry Thomassen, the father of inmate Harry, Jr., was standing outside in the jailer's office, waiting to visit his son. Thomas called to Mr. Thomassen to stop the escapee, but the father made no move against Spurgeon, who was now armed.

If released, the ten healthy inmates remaining in the jail would have been able to easily overpower the unarmed guard and lock him in a cell. Then all of the prisoners in the corridor could have escaped through the outer cellblock door when Spurgeon unlocked it. Spurgeon had promised the wounded Donnelly that he would help him escape along with the others. The problem was that Spurgeon did not know how the lever locking system at the jail worked.

Spurgeon ran back to the cellblock, shoved the pistol into Athelbert's face through the bars, and ordered the jailer to tell him how to release the prisoners in the inner tank. The young jailer noticed that the automatic pistol's safety was still on and bravely refused to obey Spurgeon's orders.

Two jail inmate trustees, Mac Osborn and John Jacobson, were working in the jail kitchen and saw what was happening. Jacobson immediately ran upstairs to the sheriff's office in the main courthouse and alerted the staff on duty there. Deputy Larry Flanagin and Deputy Emery Hess hurried downstairs to the jail. Spurgeon told the officers to stay back or he would shoot the sheriff's son. Flanagin drew his service revolver. Spurgeon squeezed the trigger, but the pistol did not fire, as he did not know how to get the gun's safety off. The two deputies wrestled the gun from Spurgeon's hand and he was forced to surrender. Authorities suspected that Donnelly had planned the escape and had used young Spurgeon to carry it out, but they could not prove this theory.

13

Sentenced to Life

AFTER A MONTH IN THE COUNTY JAIL, prosecutors decided that Mike Donnelly was strong enough to stand trial. He was charged with first-degree murder. The court appointed public defenders William P. Brown and Thomas D. Healy to represent Donnelly. County Prosecuting Attorney Frank Bixby and Deputy Prosecutor Howard Thompson would present the state's case. Jury selection began in a Bellingham courtroom on Monday, May 1, 1911. Selecting a jury proved to be difficult. After a long process of interviewing scores of prospective jurors, a final jury was selected. Donnelly appeared very interested and attentive during the entire jury selection process.

Testimony regarding Donnelly's case was heard in Superior Court for a day and a half, from the morning of May 3 until noon on May 4. Donnelly chose to take the stand and testify on his own behalf, claiming that Win Stevens had shot him first and he was only defending himself. Throughout the trial, Donnelly maintained a calm appearance.

It took the jury only a little more than three hours to bring in a verdict at the end of the day on May 4. Some doubts existed in the minds of some of the jurors what exactly had happened the day of the shootings and exactly what part doctors had played in Winslow B. Stevens' death. Because of these uncertainties, the jury handed down a verdict of guilty of murder in the second degree, rather than first-degree murder.

When deputies were bringing Donnelly back to the courtroom to hear the verdict, they characterized his demeanor as "cool." When Deputy County Clerk Frank Moses stood to read the verdict, Donnelly looked up and listened intently to the formal declaration as it was read. He laughed out loud when he heard the decision.

Judge John A. Kellogg, who presided at the trial, sentenced Donnelly on Thursday, May 11. Judge Kellogg said that, in his opinion, Donnelly should have been convicted of first-degree murder based upon apparent deliberate acts of violence in this case, and because he had demonstrated his disregard for human life by shooting at and wounding a Snohomish town marshal earlier. The judge sentenced him to the maximum penalty allowed by Washington State law for second-degree murder. Donnelly was ordered to spend the rest of his natural life in the Washington State Penitentiary.

Donnelly seemed pleased that he had escaped the death penalty. When asked how he felt about the life sentence, he said, "Oh, hell, that won't bother me any. That just means another big lumberjack in Walla Walla. I might as well be there as any place."

Entrance to the Washington State Penitentiary at Walla Walla, Washington, c. 1907. (Whitman College archives, Walla Walla, Washington)

14

A Try for Freedom

DONNELLY WAS RECEIVED AT THE STATE PRISON in Walla Walla on May 18, 1911, and was designated as Prisoner Number 6120. But he had no more intention of staying locked up in prison than he had intended to stay locked up in the Whatcom County jail. In a short time, he made his first attempt to escape from the state penitentiary.

One night, Donnelly and his cellmate managed to get out of their cell. In the corridor, Donnelly attacked prison guard Elmer A. Connick. Donnelly was then immediately jumped from behind by Thomas Clarke, an inmate trustee who was walking with the night guard. The trustee, in turn, was struck with a steel rod wielded by the second prisoner, who was trying to escape. The escapees then locked Guard Connick and Trustee Clarke in their empty cell and continued with their escape plan.

The delay caused by the unplanned scuffle in the corridor allowed time for the jailbreak to be discovered. The would-be escapees were recaptured before they could make it to the outside. Donnelly and the other convict were sent for a long stay in solitary confinement as punishment for their behavior.

15

A Successful Prison Break

THE STATE PENITENTIARY AT WALLA WALLA built a jute mill in the spring of 1911, only a month or so before Donnelly arrived at the prison. In this textile mill, the prisoners used jute imported from India to weave burlap fabric. From the fabric, the inmates sewed millions of burlap grain bags, which were then sold to the wheat farmers of eastern Washington. The prisoners made more than one million burlap bags that first year.

When released from solitary confinement, Donnelly was put to work in the prison jute mill. He cooperated and did his job, but he still had no intention of staying in prison and was biding his time until he could try again to break out. In the meantime, he made mental notes of possible avenues of escape from the large and busy textile mill—escape routes he would use if the right opportunity arose.

Finally the awaited opportunity for escape presented itself. At about four p.m. on Monday, August 14, 1911, an unexpected, severe dust storm hit Walla Walla. It was the worst dust storm in years. A cloud of dust, driven by fifty-mile-an-hour winds from the southwest, blackened the sky. Witnesses who saw the dust cloud coming said that it looked like a tornado. There were flashes of lightning within the cloud.

When the storm hit the penitentiary, acting Prison Superintendent C. S. Reed immediately ordered the prison walls surrounded with guards. The captain of the guards ran out on the wall to a position near the jute mill, where most of the inmates were working at the time. Because the dust cloud was so thick that he could hardly see his hand in front of his face, the captain made the decision that it was too dark to try to move the prisoners back to their cells.

Donnelly was working at his job in the jute mill when the dust in the air suddenly reduced visibility inside the mill to nearly zero. He took advantage of the situation. Wasting no time, he put one of his escape plans into motion. He ran right by a prison guard, who could not see him because of the thick dust. He then grabbed a ladder that was used when oiling the shafts on the textile machines. Donnelly had no problem finding the familiar ladder in the dark.

Washington State Penitentiary Jute Mill, 1911. Inmate Mike Donnelly was given a job inside the prison textile mill, where prisoners made burlap fabric from jute, to be sewn into grain bags. (Washington State Archives, Olympia, Washington)

Donnelly went into the toilet, where he had previously noted a ventilator shaft through which a person could gain access to the roof of the jute mill. He climbed through the ventilator, pulling the ladder up behind him. The ladder had hooks on one end, and he used it to descend from the roof of the building into the prison yard below.

Donnelly then headed for the outside wall of the prison, still carrying the ladder with him. The dust in the air was so thick that he could not be seen from the guard towers as he made his way across the open prison yard. On the west side of the prison, he was

Guard Tower at the Washington State Penitentiary. When Donnelly escaped from the prison jute mill, the dust was so thick that guards could not see him as he ran across the yard to the outside wall, about 100 feet from the guard tower. (Washington State Archives, Olympia, Washington)

able to reach up and hook the ladder to the top of the eighteen-foot outside wall. He scaled the wall about one hundred feet from one of the guard towers and dropped to freedom on the other side.

Although there were guards stationed outside the wall, Donnelly managed to land between guards without being detected. The dust storm created complete darkness for almost half an hour, but Donnelly did not need even that much time. He accomplished his escape in a matter of minutes.

Early in the confusion, the superintendent of the jute mill alerted the guards that possibly two men had escaped. When the dust subsided a little, the prisoners working in the textile mill were herded back into their cells and a head count and name check were taken. It was then that guards confirmed a prison break, but only one man was missing: Mike Donnelly.

By the time that the escape was discovered, Donnelly had about a forty-minute head start. From the prison, located near the northwest corner of Walla Walla, Donnelly went into the city, where he managed to steal a pair of blue overalls from someone's clothesline. The storm knocked out the telephones at the prison, so city police in Walla Walla had not yet been notified of the prison break.

Around five p.m., an hour after his escape, Donnelly—wearing the stolen pants and a dark hat that he had found—walked into Albert & Nettie Hender's grocery store at 601 Elm Street, at the corner of North Eighth Street. The store was less than a mile southeast of the prison. Ella Peaslee was working as clerk at the time. She and two small children were the only ones in the store. Donnelly went up to the counter and said that he needed to buy a shirt. The clerk thought Donnelly appeared extremely nervous. She told Donnelly that the store did not stock clothing and directed him to a nearby store that did sell shirts. He left the grocery store without saying anything more.

He was next seen a couple of blocks from the store, coming out of a woodshed at the Chris Meckleson residence at 610 West Cherry Street. He had been looking for, and found, a civilian shirt in the shed. Shortly after that sighting, authorities received a report that the escapee was seen at Magallon's Grove, the city's hobo jungle, southwest of the shed on Cherry Street. This "jungle" was located about a mile south of the prison near the Oregon-Washington Railroad & Navigation Company (O.-W.R.&N) railroad track, just north of Mill Creek. The grove was thoroughly searched Monday night by prison guards, but Donnelly was not found.

Donnelly made his way through the small grove of trees and across the O.-W.R.&N tracks to a wheat field near the west city limits. The wheat harvest was in progress, but the fugitive was able to find some tall wheat that had not yet been cut. He hid in the field, staying put until about seven forty p.m., at which time it was completely dark. The evening air was warm, nearly eighty degrees.

After dark, Donnelly walked cautiously back through the north end of Walla Walla, traveling about four miles to the eastern city limits. There was a slaughterhouse in the northeast part of Walla Walla, near the end of Isaacs Avenue, south of Butcher Creek. At about nine p.m., the escaped convict was seen by Joseph P. Stadelman, a meat cutter for the Independent Meat Company, but it was the next day before Stadelman reported that he had seen Donnelly pass by the company's slaughterhouse.

It was a clear night, and a three-quarter moon came up at about nine thirty p.m., which gave the fugitive a little light as he headed up Mill Creek, east of town. Donnelly walked all night. A young man who was arriving in Walla Walla from the east reported that he met a man hiking on a road east of the city early Tuesday morning, at about dawn. The stranger told police that the man, who fit Donnelly's description, was wearing civilian clothing and was traveling east.

Donnelly hid in another wheat field during the next day and rested. It was cloudy, but still warm, with temperatures in the upper seventies. He had water, but no food. Chewing on handfuls of wheat kernels gave him some nourishment. As soon as it got dark, he traveled again, going upstream on Mill Creek. He finally made it to the safety of the Umatilla National Forest in the Blue Mountains, at the headwaters of Mill Creek.

Donnelly stayed in the Blue Mountains for several days. In the mountains he was in an environment where he felt safe and at home. He obtained another change of clothing from a farmhouse in the area, but he did not have any real camping gear. That, however, was not a serious problem, because the temperatures were mild enough that he could make himself comfortable sleeping outside at night. His biggest problem was that he was unable to obtain enough food. He did not have a gun with which to kill game to eat. The huckleberries were ripe, and that was about all that he was able to find to sustain himself. He was afraid that he might starve to death, so he returned to Walla Walla in the same way that he had escaped—hiding in wheat fields during the day and traveling at night. He found his way back to the O.-W.R.&N.Co. railroad yard in Walla Walla, only three-fourths mile south of the prison.

Donnelly hopped a freight train that took him to Pasco, Washington. At Pasco, he crawled into a Northern Pacific boxcar, which ended up in Spokane. After hanging around the hobo jungles in Spokane for a couple of days, he hit the rails again, this time riding on the Northern Pacific line to Butte, Montana.

At Butte's higher elevation, the temperature dropped to about fifty degrees at night. It was too cold to be comfortable camping outside without any blankets, so he left the Rocky Mountains and the higher elevations of the Continental Divide after only one night.

From Butte, Donnelly rode an Oregon Short Line freight train to Idaho Falls, Idaho, where the temperatures were in the low eighties. He was becoming a regular "boxcar tourist." He had no money, so he survived in the same way as the other hobos, by begging for or stealing food and by eating wild fruits and berries that were ripe that time of year.

Donnelly was hanging around in the hobo jungle at Idaho Falls, a city with a population of 6,500, when, on August 29, he was picked up by Bonneville County Sheriff Harry C. Bucklin for questioning about a crime that had recently been committed. Donnelly was taken to the county jail, which was on the first floor of the county courthouse, located near the southwest corner of North Capital Avenue and Broadway in Idaho Falls. Donnelly told the sheriff that his name was J. T. Preston. They decided to hold him for forty-eight hours on suspicion.

When Donnelly entered the jail, there were two other male prisoners already being held in the facility. One was a young man named P. R. Christensen, who was serving ninety days for "maintaining a common nuisance." The other was Don Harriegha, who was being held as a material witness in an illegal liquor case.

After further investigation, the police could not connect Donnelly to the crime that they were investigating. They also failed to identify him as an escaped convict. Rather than release him after

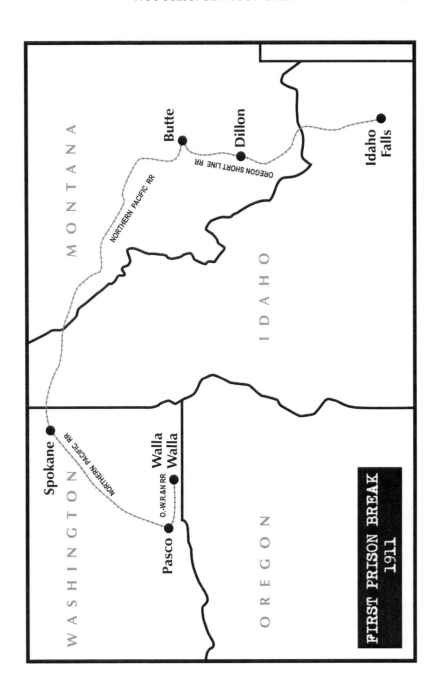

forty-eight hours, the probate court judge sentenced him to ten more days in the county jail for vagrancy, the sentence to start on August 31.

By this time Harriegha had been released, so Donnelly and Christensen were the only men remaining at the jail. According to Donnelly's own story, he confided with the other prisoner that he was an escaped murderer and that he had a life sentence hanging over his head. Donnelly said that he desperately needed to break out of jail before the police in Idaho Falls discovered who he really was. He did not want to go back to prison. Christensen promised that he would not reveal Donnelly's true identity to the jailer, nor tell anyone about his plans to escape. The young prisoner went along with Donnelly because the idea of being locked up with an over-six-foot tall, two-hundred-pound killer terrified the man, and he was not about to make his cellmate angry.

The two-story stone and brick courthouse building was wedged tightly between the *Idaho Register* newspaper office and Joseph George's restaurant. The jail in the rear of the courthouse extended beyond the buildings on either side. There was twenty-eight feet of exposed outside wall on the south side of the jail. This wall was secluded behind the restaurant and shielded from the street by piles of lumber in the Miller-Cahoon Company lumberyard on Bridge Street to the south.

Donnelly immediately went to work at chipping a tunnel through the hard jail wall. Donnelly and Christensen were alone in the jail for four days, and whenever he and his cellmate were left unsupervised, Donnelly chiseled away at the intended escape route.

On September 6, another young man named C. Miller Evans was brought into the jail on a charge of forgery. Evans accidentally discovered the hole being dug into the jailhouse wall. He immediately told the jailer.

Authorities had no idea how long the partial tunnel had been there, and Donnelly, of course, denied any knowledge of it, as did his fellow inmate, Christensen. Donnelly's captors readily accepted this friendly and cooperative prisoner's denial of doing anything wrong. Besides, jail officials reasoned, their prisoner would be released very soon, so why would he try to escape?

On September 9, Donnelly was released after serving his ten-day sentence. Police still did not realize whom they were setting free. The day after Donnelly was gone, inmate Christensen told the jailer about Donnelly's claim to be an escaped murderer with a life sentence hanging over his head. Sheriff Bucklin looked through the wanted posters in his office and he indeed found a flyer on a man wanted for escape from the Walla Walla prison. The photos and description in the flyer matched the prisoner just released. The escapee's name was Mike Donnelly. It was then that the police knew that they made a big mistake by letting an escaped murderer go free.

Sheriff Bucklin immediately sent a telegram to the warden at the Washington State Penitentiary, explaining what had happened and stating that he thought the fugitive probably had gone to Butte, Montana. The penitentiary responded by sending men to Idaho and Montana to look for Donnelly.

16
Captured in Montana

IMMEDIATELY AFTER HIS RELEASE from the Idaho Falls jail, Donnelly put some distance between himself and Idaho. He was afraid that local authorities might start looking for him again after they realized their mistake. He returned to Butte, Montana, and bummed around there for a day, but it was even colder in Butte than it had been earlier, with temperatures dropping down into the thirties at night. Wanting to get back to where it was warmer, Donnelly caught another southbound Oregon Short Line train. This time he went sixty-five miles south to Dillon, Montana. It turned out to be a poor choice.

Donnelly was rounded up with a group of transients in Dillon on Tuesday, September 12, when local deputies Joseph G. "Doc" Erwin and William T. Scully made a sweep of the hobo jungle area near the coal chutes, looking for thieves who had been stealing from the people in town. The transients were searched for possession of stolen goods. One of the men that they rounded up at the time was an ex-convict from Washington who had known Mike Donnelly in prison. That ex-con quietly revealed to the deputies Donnelly's identity as a murderer serving a life sentence, a man who had no business being out of prison. Doc Erwin and Will Scully went back to the sheriff's office and looked over the wanted posters. Sure enough, they found one with a picture and description that matched the man they saw in the jungle. They also saw on the poster that there was a $150 reward offered for the capture of this escaped murder.

When the officers returned to the hobo camp, they found Donnelly taking a dip in the Beaverhead River. Erwin went out to Donnelly and told the fugitive that he was under arrest. Donnelly lunged at the officer but missed him. Deputy Erwin drew his revolver and pointed it at Donnelly's head. The wanted man then agreed to go to jail peaceably. Thus ended Donnelly's first successful prison break. He had enjoyed almost a month of freedom—less, of course, the twelve days spent in the Idaho Falls jail.

Dillon, Montana - County Seat of Beaverhead County. On Tuesday, September 12, 1911, escaped murderer Mike Donnelly was captured by deputy sheriffs and returned to the Washington State Penitentiary. (PAC 80-61, Montana Historical Society)

17

A Second Escape

MIKE DONNELLY RETURNED TO THE PRISON in Walla Walla on September 16, 1911, accompanied by traveling guard Joseph A. Graham. Back at the prison he was taken before Warden C. S. Reed for questioning. Then, as before, he was placed in solitary confinement for punishment. He was also made to wear a shirt with red stripes to signify that he was a bad and potentially dangerous prisoner who must be closely watched.

When Donnelly was released from solitary confinement, he returned to his job at the jute mill. But this time he was housed at night in a more secure cellblock. His new cell was located in the center of the prison complex, as far from the outside wall as one could be.

Two years went by without incident. Then Donnelly made a second successful jail break. This one was well planned, and was one of the most sensational escapes in the history of the Walla Walla prison.

After supper on Tuesday evening, November 5, 1913, Donnelly slipped from a line of inmates being led from the dining room back to Cell Block No. 1, securely located in the center of the main prison building. Donnelly had earlier observed that, each day on his march back to his cell, there was a point where he was momentarily out of sight of the guards. On November 5, at this point, he jumped from the line through an open window, landing in an exercise yard below. In a matter of seconds, he climbed a standpipe to the top of the main prison building. He ran across the roof and jumped to the roof of an adjoining building. Using a rope taken from his job site in the prison jute mill that day and concealed under his clothing, Donnelly let himself down the sixteen-foot outside wall of the cell wing into the main prison yard.

The sun went down at 4:27 p.m. and there was only a quarter moon. By five p.m. that evening it was too dark to see without artificial light. Donnelly sprinted across a lighted open space for about one hundred feet to the rear of the prison hospital, where the light was poor. Two eight-foot long benches had been left outside the hospital, on which convict patients were sometimes allowed to sit in the sun. Donnelly leaned these benches against the twenty-foot outer prison wall and climbed to the top. Only ten minutes had elapsed from the time that Donnelly bolted from the line until he was missed by the prison guards, but that was time enough for him to lower himself with the rope to freedom on the outside.

Ironically, when Donnelly dropped to the ground outside the prison wall, he landed very near Warden Henry Drum's residence, located beside the prison. No one at the residence happened to see Donnelly, and he slipped away into the darkness.

When it was discovered that Donnelly was missing, prison bloodhounds were immediately put on his trail. The trail led south. The dogs were unable to stay on the escaped prisoner's scent after they got out of town into farming country. After searching all day Thursday and Friday, most of the searchers returned to the prison on Friday night, empty-handed. Donnelly had escaped again.

Immediately after his second break from prison, Donnelly looked for a hardware store in Walla Walla from which to steal a gun, but he could not find a convenient target. He did not want to stay around Walla Walla too long, so he left town unarmed.

South of town, the escapee stole a horse. Having been a farmhand and a logger in camps that used horses, Big Mike was familiar with horses and mules. To control his mount, he made a hackamore bridle from a piece of the rope taken from the jute mill. He was still carrying the rope inside his shirt. Riding bareback, Donnelly galloped away into the hills, heading southwest across Yellowhawk Creek. The hounds were not able to follow him when he was on horseback.

Donnelly rode about three miles before reaching Oregon. He

crossed Birch Creek, letting the horse pick its own way around and across ravines in the dark. After riding a total of about ten miles, he came to the Oregon-Washington Railroad & Navigation Company Railroad track between Spofford, Oregon, and Milton, Oregon. Here he abandoned his horse and climbed aboard a slow-moving freight train.

There was another man already on the train. Donnelly was still wearing prison garb, and the other transient recognized him immediately for what he was—an escaped convict. The man in the boxcar assured Donnelly that he had nothing to fear from him because he was also a fugitive. The men agreed to travel together and to help each other out. The stranger gave Donnelly a coat, a hat, and an old shirt to help hide his identity.

The pair rode the train about one hundred eighty miles west to Hood River, Oregon, a city in the Columbia River gorge with a population of about 3,800. Donnelly still wanted a gun, so in the wee hours of Monday morning, November 17, 1913, the fugitives pried open the door to Dixon McDonald's store in Hood River.

The burglars would have preferred a general hardware store to rob, but they could not find one. Dixon McDonald sold farm implements, seed, fertilizer, etc. He was also the agent for Hudson and Reo automobiles in Hood River. However, the robbers did manage to find a shotgun, a .22-caliber rifle, and a quantity of ammunition in the store They stole these firearms, along with some other small items that they thought might be useful to them later.

Mike Donnelly took the shotgun and his partner took the rifle. After leaving the store, Donnelly's partner climbed on a moving freight train. Donnelly started to hop aboard, but changed his mind. He did not really trust this stranger and felt safer traveling alone. The train carrying Donnelly's unidentified partner sped off without him. It was learned later that this man sold the stolen rifle to a resident of Cascade Locks, Oregon. With the money he was paid for the rifle, the unnamed fugitive purchased a train ticket to Portland, Oregon, and was never heard from again.

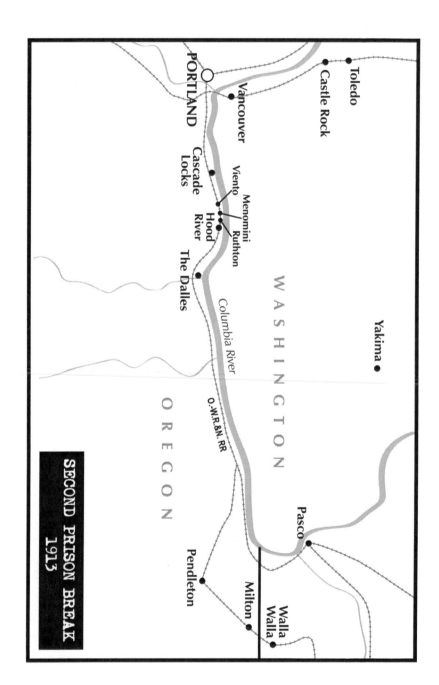

SECOND PRISON BREAK
1913

Tuesday morning, November 18, Donnelly was seen walking west on the O.-W.R.&N.Co. tracks near Menomini, four miles west of Hood River. The person who saw this stranger carrying a shotgun was suspicious and reported the sighting to authorities in Hood River. Two railroad detectives from Portland, Archie Leonard and Herb Gowen, were working in Hood River at the time. The detectives were trying to catch a gang of thieves who were systematically breaking into boxcars and stealing their contents.

On Tuesday afternoon, the two railroad detectives took a motor car and ran down the tracks to Menomini station to look for the suspect. Finding nothing at Menomini, they continued west. The detectives were beyond Menomini about a mile, near Mitchell Point, when Donnelly saw the motor car coming up behind him. Thinking the men were simply railroad workers, Donnelly sat down on the bank beside the track to let them pass. He placed the loaded shotgun across his knees.

The "speeder" stopped when it came up beside Donnelly. Donnelly was wearing the blue flannel shirt, old black coat, and dark soft hat that his former partner had given him, but the detectives noticed that he was wearing prison pants and prison boots. One of them asked Donnelly if he was going hunting, and Donnelly acknowledged that he was. The man then admired Donnelly's new shotgun and asked if he could have a closer look at it. Not wanting to arouse suspicion, Donnelly handed the man his gun. The detective checked the chamber and saw that the gun was loaded. He then pointed the shotgun at Donnelly and ordered him to get down on his stomach and put his hands behind his back. After the suspect's arms were handcuffed securely behind him, the detectives ordered their prisoner to climb aboard the motor car for the ride back to town.

The speeder met an approaching train as the party neared Ruthton, about three miles west of Hood River, and the two agents had to hurriedly set the motor car off the tracks to avoid being hit. Taking advantage of the situation, Donnelly made a run for it. He ran behind some old railroad buildings at Ruthton and then jumped into a stand of willow brush.

Leonard and Gowen ordered the prisoner to stop or they would shoot, but Donnelly took a chance and continued running. The lawmen did not realize that they had captured an escaped murderer, and they really did not want to fire at the fleeing man and possibly kill him. They thought that they could quickly overtake the unarmed, manacled suspect and return him to custody in a very short time. But, after a hard chase, Donnelly managed to elude his captors in the rugged terrain. As it would soon be dark, the detectives decided to return to Hood River.

Donnelly remained hidden until dark. He then retraced his steps and picked up his hat, which he lost in the chase. He did not want the posse to have an article of his clothing with which to give his scent to their dogs, if they should return with some. He rummaged around in a shed at Ruthton until he found an old saw. He managed with great difficulty to "chew" through the chain on the handcuffs. He could now move his hands freely, but the steel cuffs were still on his wrists.

Wednesday morning, November 19, Hood River County Sheriff Thomas F. Johnson borrowed some bloodhounds from the town of White Salmon, Washington, on the other side of the Columbia River. The sheriff, a Hood River city marshal named Joseph Kelly ("J.K.") Carson, the two railroad detectives, and the victimized store owner, Dixon McDonald, went to the place where Donnelly was last seen and began looking for him. The dogs picked up a scent, which they followed around the buildings and into the bushes for about a hundred yards. Soon the dogs went around in a circle and came back to the starting place. The dogs were put on the trail again, with the same results. Late on Wednesday, the posse returned to Hood River without their prisoner.

When they arrived back in Hood River, they learned that a store in Mosier, six miles east, had been robbed the previous night. Thinking the burglary might be the work of their suspect, the posse conducted a search east of Hood River.

Meanwhile, Donnelly had walked most of the night. On November 19, while the posse was searching for him at Ruthton, he was walking west on the railroad tracks again. Near Viento, eight miles west of Hood River, he met a railroad employee called a track walker, who was inspecting the condition of the tracks for the local section crew. Donnelly grabbed the man and showed him a bulge in his coat pocket, which he said was a pistol. He threatened to shoot the man if he did not take him to his foreman. The track walker saw the cuff on Donnelly's exposed wrist and figured that he was a desperate escaped felon, so he cooperated. The pair soon came to a group of section hands working on the tracks. It is not known what sad, hard-luck story the likable convict told, but Donnelly persuaded the sympathetic section foreman to file off his wrist bracelets.

That night, Donnelly was at Cascade Locks, eighteen miles down the railroad line west of Hood River. In the middle of the night, he broke into and robbed the Wind River Lumber Company general store at the Locks. Among the items stolen from the store were a raincoat, some flannel shirts, some pants, a pair of shoes, and a quantity of canned goods.

On Thursday morning, November 20, the incident at Viento was reported to Sheriff Johnson. When questioned, the section foreman told Johnson that a man had forced him at gunpoint to remove handcuffs from his wrists. But Johnson knew that the wanted man was not armed. He felt that the railroad workers were a little too eager to help this escaped convict, and authorities considered charging the section foreman with aiding and abetting a fugitive.

Meanwhile, Donnelly was again walking west when he met a hobo on the tracks. The two men talked awhile, but Donnelly was leery of the stranger. He had learned a lesson on his first escape from prison, when he had been picked up twice while hanging out in the hobo jungles and being friendly with the other transients. This time he intended to avoid the popular campsites and to choose his companions carefully.

Donnelly went into hiding for a few days, camping alone in the hills. Authorities thought that he probably had a camp somewhere near Cascade Locks, and the railroad company sent four of their detectives to find the fugitive. These special agents talked to the transient, who said he had had a conversation with Donnelly and that Donnelly said he was going to Portland. Railroad officials predicted that the fugitive, now confirmed to be the escaped murderer, would go south from Portland toward San Francisco, away from Washington where he was a wanted man. Unable to locate and apprehend Donnelly in the vicinity of Cascade Locks, the railroad agents concentrated their search efforts in Portland and points south.

Donnelly eventually jumped on an O.-W.R.&N. Co. freight train, which took him down through the Columbia River Gorge toward Portland. He skirted the city and crossed a bridge over the Columbia River, back toward Vancouver, Washington. He was still unarmed.

Donnelly's second run from prison lasted three months. During that time, he committed a number of holdups and robberies and was sought by law enforcement officers in several places in Washington. He became one of the most notorious outlaws ever hunted down in the Pacific Northwest. In spite of this reputation, the state penitentiary offered only fifty dollars as a reward for his capture.

18

New Sidekick Shot Dead

DONNELLY STAYED WITH HIS PLAN to avoid hanging out in the hobo jungles. However, he could not help but run into and talk to other people on the road. Around the first of December—more than three weeks after his second escape from prison—Donnelly met up with a man whose first name was Dale. Dale was not a criminal of Donnelly's class. He was dressed like a logger. Perhaps the two men had worked together in the past. At any rate, Donnelly trusted the man, and they teamed up and traveled north together.

On Thursday night, December 4, 1913, Donnelly and his new companion were in Castle Rock, a town of about 1,200 residents in Cowlitz County, Washington. Donnelly did not like being without a weapon when he was being sought by the police. He talked his new partner, Dale, into helping him rob the general store in Castle Rock, which was owned by Otto Wehtje and C.W. Dahlman. During the break-in, the pair acquired a number of firearms.

Cowlitz County Sheriff Edward Close and two of his deputies got on the trail of the Castle Rock burglars and followed them north up the Cowlitz River for about twelve miles to Toledo, a small town in Lewis County. There the sheriff lost track of the burglars. He had no description of them, but he nonetheless alerted the residents of Toledo to be on the lookout for any suspicious-appearing characters.

On Saturday morning, December 6, Mike Donnelly sent his partner into Joseph E. Steinberger's Toledo Hotel to buy some bread and other items from the hotel restaurant. Lucy Steinberger, the owner's wife, was cooking at the restaurant and agreed to sell Dale some food "to go."

Toledo, Washington - Second Street, Looking South. Mike Donnelly and his partner, Dale, two days after they robbed a store in Castle Rock, bought food at the Toledo Hotel restaurant and went into a nearby cow pasture to camp. (Lewis County Historical Museum, Chehalis, Washington)

The men took the food to a patch of woods not far from Toledo, built a fire, and set up a camp on a level spot on top of a small hill. Their camp was surrounded by brush several feet high, in a triangle-shaped piece of land where the old Chehalis-Toledo Road and the new Pacific Highway forked.

That same morning, Godfried Ritter, a Toledo butcher, went to take care of a small herd of cattle that belonged to him and his partner, Fred Weber. Ritter and Weber owned a meat market in Toledo. The cattle were pastured in that parcel of land where Donnelly and Dale were camped.

Ritter noticed the two men standing around a campfire in the brush at the upper edge of his pasture. The brush was so wet that he wondered how they'd ever got a fire started. He talked to the men, and they asked him if he had any objection to their camping on his land. Ritter, who heard about some robbers being in the area, was suspicious of the pair but did not want to frighten them off. He tried to act as if nothing was wrong, and said that he had no objections to their camping on his land, as long as they shut the gate behind them when they left.

Ritter arrived back in town shortly after noon and reported to authorities where he'd seen the two men, who could possibly be the Castle Rock burglary suspects. Sheriff Close and his deputies organized a posse of Toledo citizens to go after the wanted men.

The posse surrounded the patch of woods and slowly moved in on the men's camp above the pasture. At about three thirty p.m., fifty-eight-year-old Ex-Sheriff Ambrose F. Kirby, who had a reputation for being fearless, entered the camp to arrest the pair. Deputy Sheriff Howell backed him up. The two officers were not detected by the suspects until they were only a few feet away. A command was given for Donnelly and Dale to put their hands in the air. Instead of complying, the suspects jumped into the brush. Donnelly hit the ground with his gun blazing. Three or four bullets from Donnelly's pistol ripped through the heavy winter clothing of Deputy Howell, but miraculously the officer was not wounded. The deputies and posse members returned a barrage of fire. After the fusillade ended, Donnelly's partner stood up and started to raise his hands as if to surrender. He was shot through the chest and fell over dead.

It was almost dark by this time, and the posse lost sight of Donnelly in the woods. The officers searched the outlaw's camp and found two rifles, five revolvers, a sawed-off shotgun, several razors, and a large supply of ammunition. Otto Wehtje identified most of the recovered booty as items taken from his store in Castle Rock.

Lewis County Coroner Edward Newell was notified immediately after the shooting. He hurried from his home in Centralia to the scene. The body of the dead bandit lay right it fell. The slain man was five feet nine inches tall and about thirty years of age. He was wearing overalls, a flannel shirt, and heavy caulked boots. It was assumed that he was a logger. He was armed with revolvers and ammunition taken from Wehtje & Dahlman's store in Castle Rock. The dead man had no identification papers on him, and no one in the posse recognized him as a local resident.

The body was taken to Newell's Funeral Home in Centralia. An inquest was held and the coroner's jury, composed of six Centralia businessmen—James W. Daubney, Jack Sciutto, Will Grafton, Grover Troth, E.M. Cue, and Sid Reeves—ruled that, although it could not be determined who had actually shot the man in question, the shooting was justified. The body was held as long as possible in the hope that the remains would eventually be identified. This never happened, and the unidentified man was buried in the Mountain View Cemetery in Centralia at the expense of the county.

Lewis County Sheriff Tom Foster, whose offices were in Chehalis, was informed of the shooting incident. He and John Berry, one of his regular deputies, took Berry's automobile and the county bloodhounds and joined the other posse members in combing the woods for Donnelly. Around five p.m. the suspect was seen passing the Cowlitz Prairie Store about a mile north of Toledo. The bloodhounds were put on the trail, but the tracks were lost a short distance beyond the store. Donnelly was still headed north at the time.

The search continued at daylight, but no further trace of Donnelly could be found. The Lewis County sheriff's office called off their part of the search on Sunday evening. However, Centralia Police Chief Frank M. Roberts and Chehalis Police Chief W. C. Doyle both ordered their officers to continue a close watch for Donnelly through Sunday night and Monday. Cowlitz County officers did not abandon their chase until Monday afternoon, December 8.

On Tuesday, December 9, Special Officer Napoleon J. Provo and Prison Guard Francis H. Davis from the state penitentiary at Walla Walla arrived in Toledo to take up the search for the escaped convict, bringing two bloodhounds with them.

On Wednesday morning, the state prison officials recruited County Sheriff Foster and Ex-Sheriff Henry Urquhart—both familiar with the area—to help in the manhunt. It was believed that Donnelly doubled back on his tracks and was hiding south of Toledo, waiting for the excitement to die down. The dogs were taken to Bill Creek, where a camp had been discovered. The dogs did not pick up Donnelly's scent there, and the footprints around the camp seemed too small to be Donnelly's.

When the officers got back from Bill Creek on Wednesday night, the town of Toledo was buzzing with excitement. A suspicious-acting man had been seen around town, and later he showed up at J. T. Lewis's farm. Lewis fed the man, gave him a bed in his barn, and called the police. Sheriff Foster and Henry Urquhart went out to the farm and took the man into custody. He turned out to be only a strange-acting hobo. All other leads were cold, and the search ended on Thursday, December 11.

Washington State Penitentiary Bloodhounds. Bloodhounds were often brought in to help search for Mike Donnelly, but they never were successful in finding him.

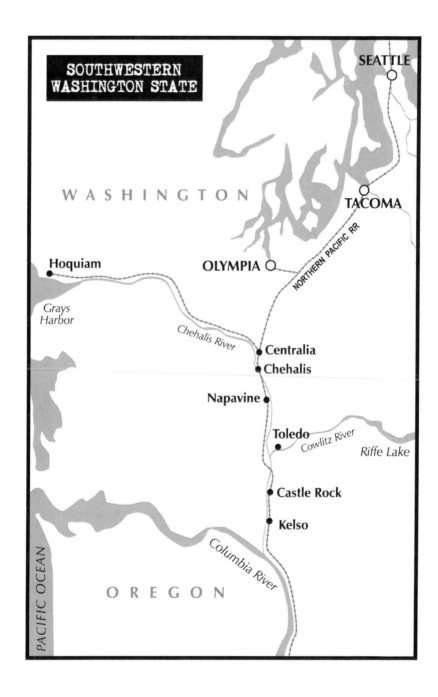

19

Fugitive Returns "Home"

FROM TOLEDO, DONNELLY WENT WEST to Grays Harbor on the Pacific Coast, where he found a couple of weeks' work in the sawmills at Hoquiam and Aberdeen. Just before Christmas 1913, he returned "home" to the general area where his criminal career had begun exactly three years earlier—an area in Washington that was very familiar to him.

Donnelly camped in the woods near Snohomish, hiding out during the day and leaving his hideout only at night. He had friends in Snohomish with whom he associated when he emerged after dark. On Monday evening, December 29, 1913, he came into town, bringing his camping gear with him. He teamed up with one of his friends to burglarize Clinton R. Sydman's hardware and sporting goods store on the south side of First Street, near the end of Avenue "A."

The back of Sydman's store overlooked the Snohomish River. Donnelly and his partner stole an old dugout canoe that they found on the bank of the river, above the Northern Pacific railroad trestle. The two burglars put their gear in the canoe and paddled it four hundred yards down the river in the dark to a point just below the store. They scrambled up the river bank and crossed the Chicago, Milwaukee & Puget Sound railroad track to the back of the store. Sydman's store was a one-story building with a basement, but the basement wall was completely exposed in the back, so it was like a two-story building on the river side.

The building beside the hardware store to the east housed the California Wine House, where Donnelly had had his first shootout with the law three years earlier. A wooden stairway led from the ground at track level up to a platform or porch on the back of the

California Wine House. The two men sneaked up the stairs at the rear of the saloon building and laid a plank from that porch to the back of Sydman's store. They had "inside information" that one of Sydman's windows had been left unlocked. They crawled across the plank to the unlocked rear window of the store. They opened the window and crawled through. This put them in a back storeroom, separated from the main store by a locked door. Tools were kept in the storeroom, so the burglars took a brace and bit and bored holes through the wooden door until one man could get an arm through and unlock the storeroom door from the other side.

They robbed the store of about $350 worth of guns and sporting goods, including two Remington pump rifles, two automatic Remington rifles, four 30-30 Winchesters, two .25-.20 Winchester carbines, one .32 special Winchester, a .12 gauge Winchester pump shotgun, a .22-caliber Colt revolver, and at least one other gun. The robbers also took six flashlights, a couple dozen leather gun holsters and cartridge belts, a dozen or more jackknives, and an extra heavy red sweater. Most of the goods were stolen to sell, but some of the things, including the sweater, were for Donnelly's personal use when he was camping.

Donnelly and his partner made several trips from the store down to the river. They loaded their loot into the stolen canoe and made their escape down the Snohomish River. The next morning when the burglary was discovered, authorities searched downriver but found no trace of the pair, who had floated the canoe all the way to Everett, Washington, about nine miles away.

Everett was the Snohomish County seat, a sizable city of nearly twenty-five thousand people. The thieves fenced most of the stolen items in Everett for some cash. Then Donnelly slipped back into hiding. He found a place to camp and hide in the woods near Marysville in Snohomish County.

The camping gear from the last robbery and his skill as a woodsman made living in his forest hideout quite comfortable, even in a cold, wet December. He continued the practice of only leaving his camp at night, occasionally venturing into Everett six miles to the south.

Authorities knew that Donnelly was in Snohomish County. People who had known him from the past reported seeing him in the area at various times throughout January 1914. But he was a very slippery character, and he easily avoided his would-be captors. With a kind of arrogance, he was not afraid to boldly steal, both to survive and to get his "kicks" by outwitting the police.

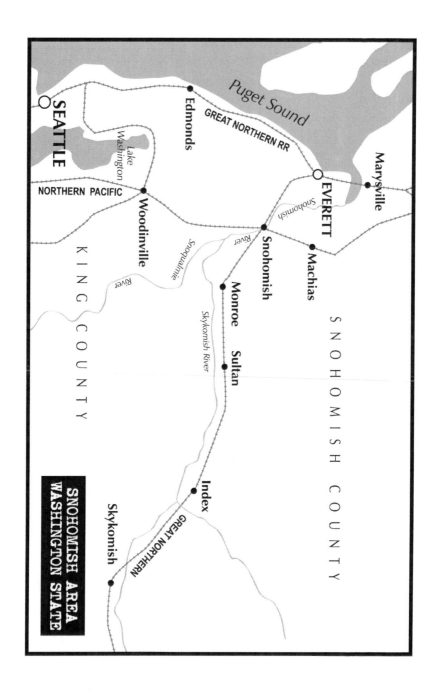

SNOHOMISH AREA
WASHINGTON STATE

20

Saloon Robbery Yields Gold

TOWARD THE END OF JANUARY, Donnelly hopped a Great Northern freight train and rode twenty-seven miles east to visit some old friends in Sultan, Washington. He went to the Sultan Lumber Company sawmill and shingle mill, three-quarters of a mile east of town, and visited night watchman Ed Harper.

Then on Saturday night, January 31, 1914, Donnelly went alone to the Capitol Saloon in Sultan, which was owned by Alexander Brown. He broke into and robbed the saloon, getting a surprising nine hundred dollars in cash, as well as some other items. Seven hundred dollars of the money taken was in gold coins. A bunch of keys was in with the money taken from the cash drawer.

Ironically, Donnelly had come full circle in the three years since he'd started his life of crime. His final saloon robbery was only a short distance from the scene of his very first saloon robbery, the holdup of McDuff & Jessup's White Front Saloon in 1910.

Immediately after robbing Brown's saloon, Donnelly went into hiding in the woods outside of Sultan to let things cool down for a couple of days. Then he started back toward his "home" near Marysville. On Wednesday, February 4, he rode a boxcar as far as Snohomish.

That night, he went to the rear of the Moehring Shoe Company store on the north side of First Street, across from the California Wine House and from Sydman's store, which he had robbed five weeks earlier.

He needed a new pair of shoes. Carefully he broke the glass in the back door, unlocked the door from the inside, and entered the store. He selected a couple of pairs of logging boots for himself. Then he stole another dozen pairs of high-topped shoes to sell. He took the shoes out of their boxes and put them into a sack. The store's owners, Charlie and Henry Moehring, reported that, in addition to seventy dollars' worth of shoes, five dollars in cash was missing from the till.

Main Street in Sultan, Washington, Looking West, c. 1914. (Monroe Historical Society)

Donnelly caught another freight train and rode to Everett. There he sold the extra shoes stolen from the Snohomish store. He spent a night in a lodging house in town before returning to his camp at Marysville.

After another week of camping in the cold rain, the fugitive decided that he was weary of the hard life that he was living. On Tuesday, February 10, he gathered up his gear and abandoned his Marysville camp. That afternoon he was back in Everett. He carried his belongings in a canvas duffel bag. He was moving to the big city of Everett, where he now had enough money to live in style.

The Moehring Shoe Store in Snohomish, Washington, Shown in Background. (Snohomish Historical Society)

21

Recaptured in Everett

WHEN HE GOT TO TOWN, Donnelly went into a saloon near the Snohomish River at the east end of Hewitt Avenue, the main commercial street in Everett, which runs between the Snohomish River and Port Gardner Bay.

At dusk, Donnelly entered the pawnshop and, for about twenty dollars each, bought two fine revolvers from Maurice Glassberg's widow, Susie Glassberg, who was alone in her store. When Donnelly left the shop, he rejoined his companions waiting outside. As the three men walked away from the store to the east, down Hewitt Avenue, Donnelly handed the package containing the handguns to one of the men.

Susie Glassberg was suspicious as she observed the behavior of the three men. A short time later, City Patrolman William D. Fee came into the pawnshop to make a routine check on gun sales for the Everett police department's records. Mrs. Glassberg told the officer about the strange gun purchase. Officer Fee called Patrolmen Arthur Johnston and Thad S. Tift for backup. The three officers set out to find the man who had purchased the handguns.

They did not have far to go. Donnelly and his companions were found in front of Nick Grad's jewelry and sporting goods store at 3005 Hewett Avenue, exactly one block east of Glassberg's pawnshop. They were drinking from a bottle of whiskey, and by this time Donnelly was a little drunk. The three policemen did not know that they were about to arrest the notorious and dangerous Mike Donnelly.

The men saw the police officers approaching. Donnelly had both hands in his pockets, and in each hand was a gun. As Officer Johnston made his move toward the suspect, Donnelly raised the

Hewitt Ave. looking East from Rucker Ave., Everett, Washington

Hewitt Avenue, Looking East from Rucker Avenue in Everett, Washington. Escaped murderer Mike Donnelly brought his camping gear into a saloon near the east end of Hewitt Avenue in Everett. (Northwest Room, Everett Public Library)

muzzle of one of the automatic pistols and squeezed the trigger. Johnston would probably have died if the pistol had not failed to discharge. The safety catch was still on. Donnelly said later that he was too drunk to get the safety off and try a second shot.

"I had a mighty funny feeling when I saw that gun sticking toward me," said Patrolman Johnston later.

Johnston leaped on Donnelly, in spite of the possibility of being shot. With one sweep of his powerful arm, Big Mike sent the husky police officer reeling into the street. The intoxicated Donnelly tried to draw another of the handguns that he carried, but Patrolmen Fee and Tift grabbed him and, after a struggle in the middle of the street, subdued him without any bloodshed. If it had not been for the fact that Officer Fee was nearly as big and strong as Donnelly, the lawmen would have had a lot more trouble taking the suspect into custody. Of course, Donnelly's drinking companions took flight when the police officers made their move.

A shackled Mike Donnelly was taken to Everett police headquarters at seven p.m. At first Donnelly denied his identity. Everett Police Chief William A. Loomis was able to confirm Donnelly's identification as an escaped murderer from the Washington State Penitentiary from Donnelly's "wanted" poster. Chief Loomis rolled up the prisoner's sleeves and exposed a tattoo in red, blue, and green on the inside of his right forearm. It was the figure of a woman in tights carrying a shield and an American flag, sitting on a spread eagle with a pennant in its mouth. The words "Young America" were on the pennant. This matched the tattoo described on the "wanted" poster. It was then that Donnelly admitted who he really was.

When Donnelly was searched, a Colt revolver and an automat-

Glassberg's Pawnshop at 2905 Hewitt Avenue in Everett, Washington. Mrs. Susie Glassberg [left] sold Mike Donnelly two handguns. She informed police, and Donnelly was captured a short time later, only a block from this store. (Northwest Room, Everett Public Library)

ic pistol were taken from his pants pockets. He had several hundred rounds of ammunition in a cartridge belt that he wore around his waist, and another Colt revolver in a holster on that belt. He also had some loose rounds of ammunition in his pockets. He had in his possession $588.30, most of it in gold coin stolen from Alex Brown's saloon in Sultan. And he had the keys and a special knife that had also been taken from Brown's saloon.

The police went to the saloon in Everett where Donnelly had been drinking earlier and retrieved his duffel bag. Inside the bag they found a high-power Remington automatic rifle which had been stolen from Sydman's store in Snohomish in December. The bag also contained Donnelly's clothing, including a white and gray mackinaw coat, logging boots stolen from the Moehring Shoe Store, and the heavy red sweater stolen from the Sydman store. Other gear that Donnelly had used while camping and hiding out in the woods was found in the bag, including a camp axe in a scabbard, a large tarpaulin, blankets, a very sharp hunting knife in a scabbard attached to a belt, and fishing tackle. Also in Donnelly's gear were a number of personal items that showed he liked to keep himself clean and well groomed: soap, a razor, a mirror, a comb, a hairbrush, and a number of colognes and other toilet articles.

The police wanted to talk to Donnelly's companions, but Donnelly refused to give the police any information. In spite of his lack of cooperation, Everett policemen Thad Tift and James D. Fox, with the help of Snohomish County Sheriff Donald McRae and Deputy Sheriff Hull, found Donnelly's three companions at ten p.m. that night. The wanted men were hiding in a boxcar at Delta, a suburb of Everett. They were arrested on suspicion of bank robbery, but did not have in their possession the two revolvers purchased from Mrs. Glassberg.

The next morning, a steady stream of people came by the city jail to see the notorious Mike Donnelly. Finally Police Chief Loomis announced that Donnelly was not on public display. Unless they had a valid reason for being there, no one was admitted to the jail cell area.

That same Wednesday morning, Everett patrolmen George English and Basil Wells recovered from an Everett saloon the two revolvers purchased from Mrs. Glassberg the night before. Apparently the hand guns had been abandoned in the saloon by Donnelly's companions after they witnessed Donnelly's arrest and realized that being associated with him would draw a great deal of unwanted attention to themselves.

Donnelly was taken to the Snohomish County jail at 3019 Rockefeller Avenue in Everett, across the street from the courthouse. Authorities there tried to get their prisoner to identify his partner who had been shot and killed in the shootout near Toledo on December 6, 1913. Donnelly refused to reveal anything about the man, other than that his name was Dale.

Donnelly said, "Dale was on the square. He wasn't a crook at all. I don't know whether he had any folks or not, but anyhow, it's better for them to hope he's living than to know he's dead."

Donnelly was asked if he had anything to do with a recent bank robbery at Granite Falls. He said that he had nothing to do with that bank robbery, but admitted he had planned to rob the bank in Marysville. The police had no way of knowing whether these statements were true or not.

As usual, Donnelly was a friendly and cooperative prisoner. He joked with his captors, suggesting to Sheriff McRae that he only be given thirty days on a chain gang for the crime of "wrestling with the police."

The sheriff said, "If I did that, could I trust you? You would probably run off and take my ball and chain with you."

Donnelly answered with a smile. "Well, if I did that, I promise I'd send them back to you by parcel post."

Washington State Penitentiary officials came to Everett to take Donnelly back to prison. Donnelly went peacefully, but vowed that he would not stay in prison long. He arrived back at the penitentiary in Walla Walla on February 15, 1914, where he was placed in solitary confinement and was again made to wear a red shirt to signify that he was a bad prisoner.

22

Convicted Murderer Paroled

IN THE FALL OF 1916, Mike Donnelly planned yet another prison break. The plan included killing guards and taking Warden Drum and his family hostage. Prison guards were tipped off that an escape attempt was scheduled to start during the showing of a motion picture in the prison chapel. This prompted the guards to conduct a surprise search of the prisoners entering the chapel. A large sledgehammer was taken from Donnelly. He was sent to "the hole" again. During his twelve-year stay in the prison at Walla Walla, Donnelly spent the equivalent of three full years in solitary confinement for his failure to comply with the rules.

After that incident, Donnelly apparently decided that the easiest way to get out of prison was to walk out the front door. On July 18, 1921, after more than three years of good behavior, he sent a long handwritten letter to the Washington State Penitentiary Parole Board, asking to be paroled. The board met in December 1921 and considered his application, but parole was denied. Donnelly applied for parole again a few months later, but in April 1922, his request was again denied.

A year later, on April 17, 1923, the prison parole board reviewed his case again. This time the board decided that Donnelly had reformed enough to be recommended for parole. He had been well behaved for more than six years. His only recent offense was talking in the dining room, for which he was punished by being confined to his cell for thirty days.

Since Donnelly was so well liked by the entire prison population, the board felt it would be a big boost to inmate morale if he were released. They hoped that other inmates would see Donnelly's early release as an example of how good behavior could be rewarded, even if a person was serving a life sentence.

Before an inmate could be released, however, there had to be a paying job waiting for him on the outside. Donnelly told the board that he had once been a sailor and that he would like to go to sea again. Although there was no evidence that he had ever been a seaman, the board believed him and found him a job on a merchant ship, a freighter sailing from Seattle to Australia.

The chairman of the parole board sent a letter to Washington Governor Louis P. Hart, recommending that Donnelly be given an Executive Parole. Donnelly received the parole order from Governor Hart on April 25, 1923. He was released on May 15, 1923, with orders to go directly to Seattle and report to a parole officer as soon as he arrived. But instead of doing as he was told, Donnelly got off the train in Seattle and immediately boarded another train bound for Spokane. In Spokane, he linked up with his old friend, Noah Arnold.

Part II

NOAH ARNOLD'S STORY
1892-1923

23

A Troubled Youth

DONNELLY'S NEW SIDEKICK, Noah Arnold, was born on February 14, 1892, in the rural community of Lowell, near Paint Lick in Garrard County, Kentucky. He was the son of Clayton A. Arnold and Mary Ann (McDonald) Arnold. His boyhood home was about nine miles east of Lancaster, the county seat, where his family owned their own small farm. Clayton Arnold also worked as a farm laborer on neighboring farms, and Mary Ann Arnold sometimes worked out of the home as a domestic servant, and took in laundry as well.

Noah was raised in a large and loving Baptist family, but he was a rebellious child. He dropped out of school after the sixth grade and began running with a wild gang of youths. In the spring of 1906, this gang robbed a place near Noah's home, and the youths were apprehended. This was undoubtedly not fourteen-year-old Noah Arnold's first criminal offense, but it was apparently the first time that he'd gotten caught.

Arnold and the other boys were indicted on a charge of grand larceny by a grand jury in Lancaster on March 12, 1906. The youths pleaded guilty. On March 14, Judge Bell committed Arnold and his friends to the Kentucky House of Reform in Greendale, about seven miles north of Lexington in Fayette County.

On December 30, 1908, after being locked up at the reform school for two years and eight months, Arnold escaped. He was sixteen years old when he broke out, and nothing had changed in his way of thinking.

After freeing himself from the reformatory, Arnold hopped a freight train on the Cincinnati, New Orleans & Texas Pacific Railroad and rode to Tennessee. Railroad detectives pulled him off the train in Memphis and charged him with illegally riding a train. The judge sentenced him to thirty days in jail, plus a $25 fine that he had to work off because he had no money. Authorities in Tennessee did not, however, identify Arnold as a runaway from a juvenile detention facility in Kentucky.

Arnold proceeded on through Mississippi and Louisiana, working at odd jobs while continuing to associate with members of the underworld. Though he was only of medium build, weighing about 153 pounds, Arnold considered himself a "tough guy." Of course, the fact that he always carried a firearm gave him the confidence to act tough. According to Arnold's own story, he shot and killed more than one person during this period of his life, but the details of these shootings are unknown.

Three years after he ran away from the reformatory, nineteen-year-old Arnold returned to the part of Kentucky with which he was most familiar. At this time he partnered up with a local young man named Will Burley. The pair took up residence in a barn only seventeen miles east of the Kentucky House of Reform.

Around ten p.m. on Thursday, January 4, 1912, only a short time after Arnold's return to Kentucky, he and Will Burley used a crowbar to pry open one of the windows in James W. Mallory's general store at Glen Kenney Station, about four miles from Paris, Kentucky. The burglars entered the store and carried away a quantity of merchandise, including tobacco, shoes, clothing, razors, knives, a .22-caliber rifle, and a .38-caliber pistol.

The robbery was discovered early Friday morning. Deputy Sheriff William F. Talbott was called to the scene. He contacted the city police captain in Lexington, Volney K. Mullikin, and borrowed a bloodhound from Captain Mullikin's kennel. The hound followed a trail from Mallory's to a nearby house and barn. In the barn the police found evidence of where the men had been staying and sleeping in a pile of straw.

Chief of Detectives Malcolm Brown was put on the case. He quickly identified Will Burley as one of the burglars and traced him to Lexington. Detective Brown, along with detectives Thomas F.

Donlen and James Stewart, arrested Burley in Lexington on Tuesday, January 9, 1912. Burley confessed to the crime and revealed the identity of his partner to the police. Arnold was arrested in Lexington later that same day. At the time of his arrest, he was armed with the stolen .38-caliber pistol.

The burglars were brought to the Bourbon County Courthouse in Paris, Kentucky, on Wednesday morning, where they appeared before Judge Denis Dunden. Both men pleaded guilty to charges of burglarizing the store. In lieu of bail of two hundred and fifty dollars each, they were held in the county jail until the March term of the Bourbon Circuit Court.

Arnold and Burley were brought before the grand jury in Paris on March 15, 1912. Both were indicted for breaking into the store. They pleaded guilty to the charge of second degree burglary. On March 18, the judge sentenced both Arnold and Burley to confinement at hard labor in the state penitentiary for an indeterminate period of not less than one year nor more than five years.

On Friday, April 19, 1912, Bourbon County Sheriff Albert S. Thompson transported Arnold, Burley, and two other prisoners to the Kentucky State Penitentiary in Frankfort. The sheriff and his prisoners were accompanied by Bourbon County's Head Jailer Joseph A. Farris and Deputy Sheriff Rudolph Davis. At the penitentiary, Arnold was turned over to the care of Warden Edward E. Mudd and was designated as Prisoner No. 3377.

Arnold's behavior at this correctional facility was not good. He was punished a number of times for fighting and for refusing to work. Because of his bad conduct record, his stay in prison was longer than would normally have been necessary.

After Arnold served the first mandatory year, parole was denied because he did not appear to be ready for release. His behavior worsened. On January 29, 1914, he got into trouble for fighting with another inmate. Two days later, he was placed in solitary confinement for a day for refusing to work.

On April 29, 1914, he got into a fight again. This time he was placed in solitary confinement for three and a half days for trying to cut another inmate named Smith. Ten days after he was let out of "the hole," he was put back into solitary for three hours for fighting again.

Arnold served nearly three years in prison before he began complying with the rules long enough to be paroled on February 18, 1915. Upon his release from prison, he immediately violated the conditions of his parole by leaving Kentucky and going to Chicago.

He worked at odd jobs in Chicago for about a year. Then, in the spring of 1916, he was arrested on suspicion of being connected to a shooting in Chicago. When Arnold was fingerprinted and released, he was afraid that authorities would trace him back to Kentucky and find out that he was wanted for parole violations, so he ran.

He climbed into a boxcar on a westbound freight train on the Chicago, Burlington & Quincy Railroad and rode to St. Paul, Minnesota. In St. Paul he stowed away on a Northern Pacific train and headed west, intending to ride all the way to the coast.

In Staples, Minnesota, Arnold was pulled off the train and arrested for vagrancy. After being fingerprinted, he was released and given twenty-four hours to get out of town. His identity from the fingerprints was learned too late for the authorities in Minnesota to detain him.

Arnold was picked up again in Missoula, Montana, as a suspect in a crime. He was cleared of that crime, but was sentenced to ten days in jail for vagrancy. The sentence was again suspended with the understanding that he would continue "down the line" and not hang around town.

Arnold's travels west took him through the towns of Hope and Sandpoint, Idaho, and Spokane, Washington. In June 1916, a couple of weeks after leaving Chicago, he arrived in Tacoma, Washington, more than twenty four hundred miles from his home in Kentucky.

24

Trouble Comes to Tacoma

SOME WEEKS PRIOR TO ARNOLD'S ARRIVAL in Tacoma, the longshoremen's union went on strike all up and down the Pacific Coast. The strike was settled with an agreement signed on June 9. However, on June 22 the longshoremen in Tacoma, as well as other dock workers along the entire Pacific seaboard, walked off the job again, tying up shipping on the West Coast. Emotions ran high, and a riot was staged by striking dock workers on the Sperry Flour Company docks in Tacoma on Monday night, June 26.

Arnold took advantage of the situation. He crossed the picket lines and got a job as a "scab" dock worker—a strike breaker. He went to work on Pier 3, a city dock under the supervision of Tacoma's Commissioner of Public Works, Hamilton F. Gronen. The strike did not end until the first week of October, and Arnold worked on the docks for about two and a half months.

During the lunch hour on Friday, September 29, 1916, Arnold was engaged in a game of dice with some fellow workers at the Milwaukee Oriental Dock, located on the tide flats near the town of Fife. A few minutes before one o'clock, Arnold got into an argument over the game with a man named Phillip Rucker. When the angry man lunged at Arnold, the latter pulled a .38-caliber revolver and fired one shot, narrowly missing Rucker's head. The bullet lodged harmlessly in the hull of a Japanese freighter, the *Shosen Maru*, which was tied up at the dock. Police were called, and Police Chief Smith hauled Arnold off to the Tacoma City Jail.

Phil Rucker came to police headquarters on Saturday, September 30, and filed a complaint against Arnold, who was using the alias "Robert Ford." The case was called at ten a.m. that same day.

The defendant was brought before City Police Judge DeWitt M. Evans. James W. Selden, deputy prosecuting attorney for Pierce County, charged Arnold (Ford) with assault with a deadly weapon with intent to kill. Arnold was arraigned and pleaded guilty to the lesser charge of assault in the third degree. In lieu of posting bond, he was ordered bound over in the county jail to await sentencing.

On October 6, Arnold was brought before Superior Court Judge Ernest M. Card, who sentenced him to six months in the Pierce County jail, where he was designated as Prisoner No. 2304. Curiously, Arnold only served thirty days of that sentence before Phil Rucker, the man at whom he had shot, petitioned the court to have Arnold's sentence partially commuted.

Not long after getting out of jail in November, Arnold got into an argument with a woman in Tacoma. Definitely too quick on the trigger, he ended up firing shots at the woman. Fortunately for her, he did not hit her. Police were called and Arnold claimed that the woman shot at him first. The exact details of that incident have not been learned. While police were investigating, Arnold left Tacoma to avoid prosecution. He went to Seattle and took a room in the Yorozuya Hotel at 655 Main Street, which was owned by Kakutaro Watanabe.

25

A Killing Leads to Prison

LIVING IN THE YOROZUYA HOTEL at the same time as Noah Arnold was a woman named Mabel Beale and her common-law husband, Harry Agee. Agee was a barber at the Rex Hotel on the corner of Seventh Avenue and King Street, and Mabel was a manicurist. It was not long before Noah Arnold and Mabel Beale became "friendly."

On Thursday, January 4, 1917, Beale invited Arnold up to her room. Harry Agee came home some time after eleven p.m. that night and found Arnold with his wife. Agee was angry and threatened Arnold.

Arnold ran out of the room, into the hallway, and up a little stairway. Agee followed him to the doorway, cursing him and calling him names. Arnold stopped and turned on the stairs, drawing his pistol.

"What is that you called me?" he said.

Without waiting for an answer, trigger-happy Arnold shot thirty-five-year-old Harry Agee through the head, killing him instantly. His body fell, straddling the doorway between his apartment and the hallway.

Tenants in the building heard the shot and came running out of their rooms. Patty Schwartz, daughter of hotel employee Mrs. Albert Schwartz, was one of the people at the scene. Mabel Beale asked Miss Schwartz to call an ambulance, which the girl did. Then Mrs. Schwartz, the girl's mother, called the police. Mabel Beale disappeared before the police arrived. She was last seen running down the steps of the hotel.

When Seattle City Physician Dr. Josiah Millett arrived at the scene, he pronounced Harry Agee dead. Police began looking for the shooter and for Agee's live-in girlfriend. At the time, the motive for the killing was unknown.

Mabel Beale was apprehended Friday morning. When questioned by police, she said that a strange man wearing a black and white hat had been lurking in the hallway outside the room. She said that the stranger had shot Harry Agee when Agee went to the door to investigate a sound that they'd heard. However, further questioning of the tenants in the hotel revealed that Beale had a boyfriend living at the hotel, who had disappeared right after the shooting.

Arnold fled back to Tacoma, but was hunted down by police and arrested four days later. He was charged with second-degree murder. Still using the alias "Robert Ford," he pleaded not guilty. Seattle Attorney C. L. Grey was appointed to defend him.

The trial was held in King County Superior Court on April 10, 1917, with Judge John M. Ralston presiding. Arnold's attorney claimed that Arnold had acted in self- defense and so was not guilty of a crime. Prosecutor Alfred H. Lundin argued that since Agee was not armed, Arnold was hardly in any danger. The prosecutor further contended that Arnold was the kind of person who always carried a gun, and his past record demonstrated that he was "altogether too willing to shoot."

The prosecution wanted a conviction for second-degree murder. The jury, however, convicted Arnold of the lesser crime of manslaughter. On April 28, Judge Ralston sentenced him to no less that two years and no more than twenty years in jail.

"Robert Ford" (Noah Arnold) was first sent to the State Reformatory in Monroe, Washington, where he was received from King County on May 9, 1917, as Prisoner No. 2197. Arnold was soon involved in a fight with another inmate. Later there was a riot in the dining room in which Arnold was thought to be involved. It turned out that he was not one of the men who started the riot. But when it was learned "Robert Ford" was actually Noah Arnold and that he had prior convictions in Kentucky and was wanted there for parole violations, authorities decided that Arnold was not suited for a reformatory setting. He was transferred to the Washington State Penitentiary at Walla Walla.

Arnold was received at the state penitentiary on December 7 as Prisoner No. 8432. There he went to work as a laborer in the prison jute mill, where he met and befriended convicted murderer Mike Donnelly, also a laborer in the mill.

Arnold was fairly well behaved during his stay in the penitentiary. When the parole board met on December 12, 1921, they decided to grant Arnold a parole. On April 4, 1922, barber Frank J. Buckley offered him employment as a porter in Hugh McElroy's barbershop at 328 W. Riverside, near the Chamber of Commerce building in Spokane, and Arnold was released. He went to live in Spokane, where he was assigned to a parole officer.

Arnold's bad temper was soon getting him into trouble again and he lost his job at the barbershop. He was employed for a while at two other places in Spokane, but he did not work out on those jobs, either. He soon stopped reporting to his parole officer, and the system lost track of him. Arnold ended up living on the streets of Spokane for several months before teaming up with Mike Donnelly.

Part III

CRIME SPREE IN 1923

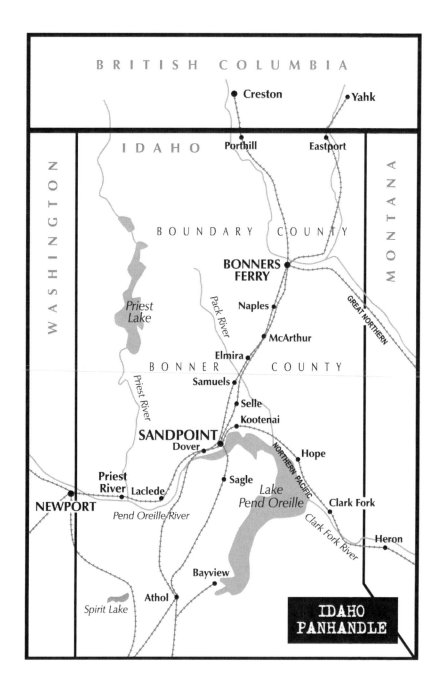

26

"Gun Play" in Northern Idaho

AFTER THE TWO EX-CONS got together again, they hopped an eastbound Northern Pacific freight train in Spokane. Both were armed with pistols and intended to "live by the gun," with little regard for the law or the rights and safety of others. After riding about seventy-five miles, Donnelly and Arnold got off the train in Bonner County, Idaho.

The Sloan & Hastings Construction Company of Spokane had a contract to widen and improve the state road through the rock cuts on the east side of Lake Pend Oreille in Bonner County. The company had a construction camp on Trestle Creek, which flows into the lake on its east side. Shortly after the supper hour on the evening of Wednesday, May 30, 1923, Donnelly and Arnold boldly held up this road-building crew in their camp.

The two men entered the camp wearing handkerchief masks. At gunpoint, they made the twelve construction workers line up in a row. While one robber covered the workers with a revolver, the other went through the workmen's pockets and took about fifty dollars in cash and several watches. They then escaped into the hills to the northeast above the creek.

The next night, Thursday, May 31, at eleven p.m., the night clerk at the Ponderay Hotel on the corner of Fourth Avenue and Cedar Street in Sandpoint, Idaho, noticed Arnold pass in front of the hotel on the Cedar Street side. At the corner, he turned and entered the hotel lobby through the Fourth Avenue entrance. Donnelly, in the meantime, positioned himself as a lookout near the Cedar Street entrance. The clerk saw Donnelly looking in through one of the large front windows of the lobby.

Ponderay Hotel at Fourth Avenue and Cedar Street in Sandpoint, Idaho. This later photo of the Ponderay Hotel shows the hotel very much as it was on the night of May 31, 1923, when it was robbed by Noah Arnold and Mike Donnelly. (Bonner County Historical Museum)

Arnold was wearing a blue serge suit and a blue dress shirt. He appeared fairly well dressed except for the old pair of shoes on his feet. He had a dark hat pulled down over his face, but he was not wearing a mask.

The night clerk, thirty-year-old James R. Hewett, saw the stranger approaching the desk with his hands clasped. As he neared the counter, he uncovered his left hand, which held a .38-caliber revolver. Arnold pointed the gun at Hewett and forced him to open the cash register. Arnold then went behind the cigar counter and rifled the cash drawer. He got nineteen dollars in silver, five dollars in currency, and a traveler's check signed by Olga Sandstrom. Arnold fled back out the Fourth Avenue door and ran in front of the hotel on Cedar Street. He joined his partner, Donnelly, and both bandits ran north on Third Avenue.

Hewett telephoned the Bonner County sheriff's office, which in turn called the city police station. Responding to the call were County Sheriff William Kirkpatrick, city night patrolman Matt Benson, and special police officer David Ryan. Given a description of the suspects, the officers split up to search for them. Officer Benson made the rounds of all alleys and hiding places in the Sandpoint business district. Officer Ryan drove Sheriff Kirkpatrick to the north end of Third Avenue and dropped him off at the west end of the Humbird Lumber Company footbridge across Sand Creek. Then he raced his car back through town, across the Cedar Street Bridge, and north along the railroad tracks to the village of Kootenai, where he positioned himself to watch for the suspects.

It was drizzling rain as Sheriff Kirkpatrick made his way across the Humbird footbridge. When he reached the east end of the bridge, he saw a shadowy form near the "Four L" union hall, where the Loyal Legion of Loggers and Lumbermen, Local 89, held their meetings and social events. The sheriff commanded the person to halt and was answered by a revolver shot. The figure disappeared into the darkness before the sheriff could return fire. For a short distance south, Kirkpatrick walked cautiously in the direction that the shadow had fled.

Near one of the warehouses just west of the Northern Pacific train depot, Sheriff Kirkpatrick shone his flashlight on the man he was following. Revolver drawn, the sheriff was approaching Noah Arnold when Mike Donnelly slipped up behind him, placed a .38-caliber revolver against his back, and fired. The bullet entered Kirkpatrick's back on the right side and came out a few inches from the hip joint. The shock of the bullet dazed him, but he did not fall. The bandits laughed and moved off into the darkness.

The shooting occurred shortly after midnight. A few minutes later, the driver of a car traveling from Sandpoint to Kootenai saw the wounded sheriff, picked him up, and took him back to City Hospital in Sandpoint. The sheriff, although in considerable pain, was able to walk from the car into the hospital. When nurses put him into a hospital bed, they found the spent bullet in the folds of his clothing.

At three a.m. Friday morning, Dr. Ones F. Page, assisted by Dr. N. R. Wallentine, performed exploratory surgery on Sheriff Kirkpatrick and determined that the bullet had not hit any vital organs as it passed cleanly through his body. They washed the wound with antiseptic and made the sheriff as comfortable as possible.

In the meantime, a number of posses were organized to patrol and guard area roads, bridges, railway stations, and yards. Besides all of the freight trains, at least fourteen passenger trains arrived and departed at Sandpoint each day. For the next couple of days all trains entering and leaving the city were closely inspected. Some thought the bandits may have slipped through the net and escaped, but most people believed that both men were hiding near the city, because it would be almost impossible for them to leave by public transportation without being detected.

On Sunday afternoon, it was reported that two men fitting the descriptions of the holdup men were sighted at Samuels, about ten miles north of Sandpoint. Deputy Sheriff Ralph H. Decker, Ray Jagger, Pete Schainstine, and Sandpoint Fire Chief Winfield P. Francis covered the territory around Samuels, traveling in two automobiles. But no one saw the suspects.

While the deputies were searching around Samuels, the eastbound local passenger train coming out of Sandpoint passed by. Deputy Decker drove his car at great speed northward along the Great Northern railroad track to Elmira. He stopped the train at Elmira and searched it inside and out, top to bottom. When the train left, he drove quickly to intercept the same train at McArthur to search it again. He then raced this train as far north as Naples, where he searched it a third time. His searches turned up nothing.

Despite unceasing efforts to find the suspects, they were still at large on Monday morning, June 4, when the search was finally called off. Cities and towns throughout the Northwest were notified and a number of potential suspects temporarily detained, but the real bandits were not captured.

In fact, Donnelly and Arnold had gone into hiding immediately after shooting Sheriff Kirkpatrick. In the wee hours of Friday morning, right after the holdup, the two men walked northeast on the Northern Pacific track from Sandpoint to Kootenai, a distance of three miles. Somehow they had avoided detection by Officer Dave Ryan on his search through that area. They left the tracks and

Humbird Lumber Company Footbridge on Sand Creek at Sandpoint, Idaho. It was drizzling rain when Sheriff William Kirkpatrick came across this bridge from "Milltown" in the distance. He was following the men who just robbed the Ponderay Hotel. (Bonner County Historical Museum)

made camp about a mile north of Kootenai, near a waterhole on a steep, wooded ridge that jutted out of the farmland in the valley. The outlaws wisely stayed put rather than trying to escape on one of the many passing trains.

On June 5, after things quieted down, the two men left their hideout and started walking east along the Northern Pacific track, away from Sandpoint. On the Oden Bay side of Kootenai Point, on a wooded hill, they found an old, abandoned cabin. The hill, at that time called Boyer Hill, was on the north shore of Lake Pend Oreille and the east side of Boyer Slough. The pair spent the night in this shack. The next morning, they caught an eastbound freight, landing in Plains, Montana, on June 7. They were now a little more than a hundred miles from Sandpoint. After looking around Plains, they began making plans to rob the bank there.

27

Bank Robbery in Montana

EARLY ON THE MORNING OF JUNE 8, the robbers went undetected to the Farmers and Merchants State Bank of Plains, on Main Street between the drug store and the post office. They wanted to learn the bank's routine, such as the time that the first employee arrived in the morning, how that person entered the bank, etc. Later, after the bank had opened for business, Arnold went inside to study the conditions there. He did nothing to disguise himself and was seen by a number of people. That afternoon, the two men walked southeast out of town, along the railroad tracks, toward the town of Paradise to choose an escape route and decide where they would meet up after the robbery.

Farmers and Merchants State Bank of Plains, Montana. The bank, located between the drugstore and the post office, was robbed on the morning of June 11, 1923, by Noah Arnold and Mike Donnelly.
(PAC 98-67.2, Montana Historical Society)

On Saturday, Arnold went to Vacura Motors, the local Ford dealer in Plains, and made arrangements with the owner, Louis Vacura, to be driven to Paradise some time between nine and ten a.m. Monday morning. Arnold paid Vacura three dollars in advance for the ride. On Sunday, Arnold again allowed himself to be seen by going into a local grocery store and buying bread, bologna sausage, and other items for use in his planned getaway into the hills after the robbery.

Late Sunday afternoon, a severe windstorm hit western Montana. Winds on Flathead Lake were clocked at forty-three miles per hour. Trees all over the area were uprooted and broken off. About twenty miles south of Plains, at Rivulet, falling trees demolished the general store. A tornado-like wind in that area twisted off trees and killed two lumberjacks in a logging camp. Communication by wire was knocked out to Northern Pacific stations up and down the line, including Plains and Paradise.

Early Monday morning, June 11, while it was still dark, Donnelly and Arnold went to the back of the Farmers and Merchants State Bank. They cut the telephone wires so that those inside would not be able to call for help during the robbery. Then they waited in hiding behind the building.

Around eight a.m., Cashier George W. Larse came to work and unlocked the back door of the bank. Larse entered the bank, and Arnold slipped in behind him without being seen. Donnelly stayed in hiding outside as a lookout, just as he had done at the holdup of the Ponderay Hotel in Sandpoint eleven days earlier. Donnelly told Arnold that, if something went wrong, Arnold was to flee out the back door and Donnelly would cover him with his revolver. Arnold was really taking all of the risk.

Inside, Larse prepared for the day's business. At about eight thirty a.m., when he returned to the back room where Arnold was hiding, the robber confronted the cashier with a revolver and ordered him to open the vault. Larse explained that the vault could not be opened until nine a.m. because of a time lock. Arnold made Larse sit in one chair while he nervously sat in another chair, holding the pistol.

When the vault lock released, Arnold pushed Larse toward it, removing the bank's pistol from under the counter so that it could not be used against him. At gunpoint, Larse was forced to work the combination to the vault.

He stalled in every way that he could, knowing that the bank president would soon be coming to work. Arnold became impatient with Larse's fumbling. He shoved the gun into the cashier's back and told him to hurry or he would pull the trigger.

When the vault door opened, Arnold pushed the cashier into the vault, tripping him facedown on the floor. He quickly bound Larse's hands and feet with ropes that he had in his pockets. From a shelf in the vault Arnold picked up a package of Liberty bonds worth more than $10,000. But when the cashier convinced the bandit that the package he held contained only old canceled notes, the valuable bonds were dropped to the floor. Arnold then grabbed all the cash that was within his reach and threw the coins and currency into a satchel he'd brought with him. The inexperienced bank robber even took a bag of nickels, which added more than three and a half pounds to the weight of his bag, but only netted him sixteen dollars.

Just as Arnold finished gathering up the money, Bank President Charles S. Robinson unlocked the front doors and came into the bank. Arnold rolled Larse onto his back and gagged him by placing a heavy ledger book over his face and another ledger on his chest. Robinson saw that the outer door to the vault was open and went inside to investigate. Arnold confronted Robinson with the bank's own pistol and ordered him onto the floor where Larse lay. Arnold bound Robinson's hands, then picked up the bag of money and slung it over his shoulder. He closed the vault door, locking the two bankers within.

Then Arnold peeled off the blue overalls that he was wearing and stuffed them into his satchel. He was wearing a brown suit underneath. He ran out the back door of the bank, carrying between $1300 and $1500 in cash. Burdened by his heavy load of cash,

food, and clothing, Arnold calmly walked across the street in front
of the bank to the nearby garage where Louis Vacura was waiting
to drive him to Paradise, six miles away. Vacura, of course, had no
idea that the bank had just been robbed.

At a spot between Plains and Paradise called "Double Crossing"
(because the highway crossed from one side of the railroad tracks
to the other, then back again), Arnold told Vacura to stop the car
and let him out. They were near Clark Cone's cattle ranch, and Arnold told Vacura that he wanted to see someone at the ranch. After
leaving the car, Arnold quickly disappeared into the brush on the
side of the road. Vacura thought this behavior was very strange and
was sure that Arnold was up to something. He returned to Plains,
where he learned that the bank had been robbed. He immediately
suspected his strange-acting passenger.

Meanwhile, Arnold buried the heavy gold, silver, and other
coins. With the currency and supplies left in his pack, he ran up
a steep draw that went about three miles northeast to the top of a
ridge near the headwaters of Henry Creek.

Donnelly, in the meantime, slipped away from the bank without being seen. However, several people had seen Donnelly and
Arnold together during the prior few days. After the bank robbery
was discovered, the police knew to be on the lookout for a second
man besides Arnold. Quickly, before a posse began checking trains,
Donnelly rode a freight train up the Clark Fork River through Paradise and beyond. Donnelly dropped off of the train somewhere
between Perma and Dixon.

A short time after Arnold left the bank, Robinson and Larse
were able to untie each other. There was a ventilation system in the
bank vault, so the bankers were not in danger of suffocation. There
were also tools inside the vault for just such an emergency as this.
Robinson and Larse were able to remove a plate from the vault door
and set the tumblers to open, but they needed someone to actually
turn the handle on the outside of the door. The men were rescued
from the vault by patrons who came into the bank to do business
and heard them knocking on the vault wall. With the trapped men

calling out instructions, the patrons turned the latch on the door and set them free.

The sheriff in Thompson Falls, twenty-five miles to the west, was notified immediately of the bank robbery. Word also spread quickly through the small town of Plains.

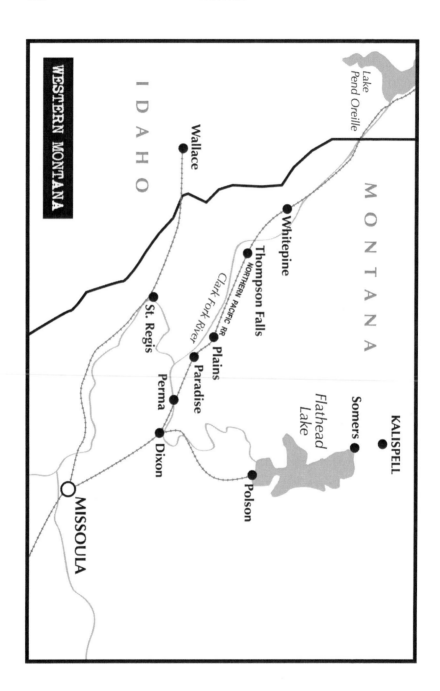

28

Eluding Another Posse

AS SOON AS SANDERS COUNTY SHERIFF Perry A. Heater was notified of the bank robbery in Plains, he deputized a large number of citizens to form a posse. Garage owner Louis Vacura was also deputized as a member of the posse and led them to the place where he'd dropped off the man believed to be the bank robber. The men spread out into the hills to look for the suspect.

Additional posse members were assigned to guard all of the stations along the Northern Pacific Railroad in the vicinity of Plains. Communication with law officers in other towns was difficult because telephone and telegraph lines were still down from Sunday's storm.

Thirty-two-year-old Virgil A. McKnight, a local rancher, and sixty-one-year-old John A. Peterson, a watchman for the Northern Pacific Railroad, were two of the posse men pursuing Noah Arnold. These two citizen lawmen caught up with the wanted man on a mountain trail near the headwaters of Henry Creek. Peterson was in front of McKnight on the trail, and when Arnold heard him coming, he stepped off of the trail and waited in ambush. When Peterson came within ten feet of Arnold's hiding place, the fugitive stepped out of the brush with his revolver aimed at Peterson, who threw up his hands. Just then, Deputy McKnight came into sight and hollered at Arnold to drop his gun. The startled bank robber turned and fired several quick shots at the approaching deputy. The second bullet from Arnold's pistol hit McKnight in the right cheek, chipping his jaw. Arnold turned and ran. Peterson drew his weapon, but his automatic pistol malfunctioned when he tried to shoot Arnold. Peterson could not get the jammed pistol to work, and the fugitive escaped into the heavy brush and timber.

Deputy McKnight was dazed but conscious. When he regained his composure, he was able to walk out to the road with the help of his partner. McKnight was taken to Plains for treatment. His wounds were not serious.

Bloodhounds from the Montana State Penitentiary at Deer Lodge were recruited to aid in the search. On Tuesday morning, with reinforcements in place, an attempt was made by the now forty-man posse to surround the ridge between Henry Creek and Camas Creek. It was believed that Arnold was trying to get to the Camas Prairie Basin and Dog Lake, about six miles northeast of the place where he was last seen. A road from that point led into some of the most inaccessible terrain on the Flathead Indian Reservation. The dogs and the posse could not pick up the trail, but they did not give up. They continued searching all day Wednesday in the rain.

A man fitting the description of the second suspect reportedly purchased some ammunition and other supplies at the town of Whitepine. He was tracked to his cabin near Belknap and arrested. The man was soon released when he proved where he was at the time of the bank robbery.

Not a single clue was found by the posse combing the hills between Plains and Paradise. On Thursday, after the Camas Prairie country was searched without a trace, the posse men started returning from the search area, a few at a time.

These returning posse men were correct when they speculated that the bank robber must have made his way back to the railroad tracks, possibly at Dixon, and that he probably caught a Northern Pacific train to parts unknown. However, the sheriff disagreed. He felt that the man they were looking for could not possibly have escaped. Sheriff Heater and twelve deputies continued the search on Friday, June 15, but finally they, too, had to give up.

Arnold did not continue up and over the ridge where he was last seen. Instead, he turned south, staying on the ridge top until he reached the head of Clear Creek. He headed east down Clear Creek ten miles to Camas Creek. Tuesday had been nice and warm, but it started raining on Wednesday as he followed Camas Creek back to the Clark Fork River. He crossed the bridge at Perma, to the south side of the Clark Fork, and made his way down the Northern Pacific track toward Dixon. There Arnold got back together with his partner, Mike Donnelly.

Donnelly and Arnold knew that a world championship heavyweight boxing match between champion Jack Dempsey and challenger Tommy Gibbons was scheduled to take place in Shelby, Montana, on the Fourth of July. The fight meant there would be large crowds of strangers in town, among whom the wanted men would merely be two more faces. These bank robbers also had lots of money, which meant that they could go to the fights and celebrate in style. They talked it over and made a decision to travel northeast to the oil boomtown of Shelby.

A Northern Pacific freight train took the pair to the town of Polson at the south end of Flathead Lake. They bought some supplies and then took their time hiking and camping during a forty-mile trek around Flathead Lake to Somers, on the north end of the lake near Kalispell. The weather was cloudy with rain showers, but it was not really too cold for camping out. Donnelly was again in his element and loving it. He was very much "at home" camping in the wilds. It was about June 21 when the fugitives hopped a Great Northern freight train near Kalispell that took them over the Continental Divide all the way to Shelby.

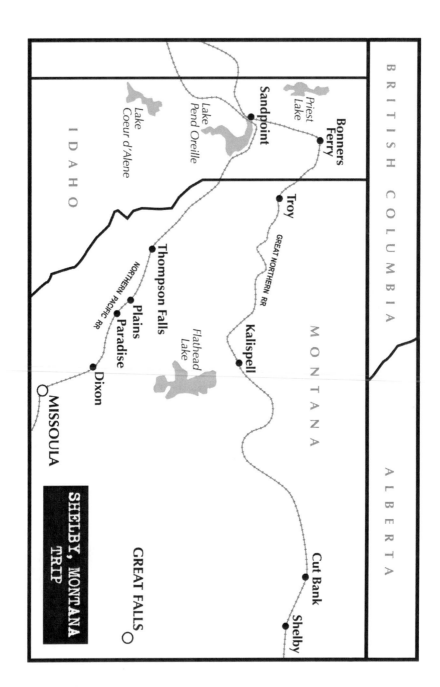

29

"Holiday" in Shelby

THE OUTLAWS GOT TO SHELBY more than a week before the Fourth of July. They had to hide out in the pouring rain until the crowds started arriving for the big fight. While waiting for fight day, the pair obtained some better camping gear and replenished their supplies by burglarizing and robbing several businesses in Shelby.

Shortly before the Fourth of July, the heavyweight championship fight was called off. Then, after some negotiations, fight promoters announced that the fight was on again. Then it was off again. Finally, it was on again, just twenty-four hours before it had been scheduled to take place. This was not enough notice for fight fans from the east or other faraway points to get to Shelby; therefore, the crowds were smaller than anticipated.

The weather cleared, and on the day of the fight there was a blazing sun and not a breath of wind. The boxing event was held in an outdoor arena. The best seats cost twenty dollars each. On the morning of the fight, only about ten thousand tickets had been sold. Just before fight time, the price of a ringside seat was cut by fifty percent, but even so, there were still plenty of empty seats. Large crowds gathered outside, but they were not buying tickets.

After the fight started, the cheap seats went on sale at much less than half price. The poorer people started coming in. Finally the seething crowd outside "crashed the gates" and poured into the arena, filling the empty seats. An estimated twenty-five thousand fans watched the fight inside the sun-baked arena, but most of these people did not purchase tickets. In the end, fight promoters lost about $48,000 on the event, and Montana businessmen lost another $32,000.

Fans saw two preliminary fights before the championship fight. In the main event, Tommy Gibbons was the underdog, but he was the big favorite of the crowd. During most of the fight, Gibbons was on the defensive. However, the fact that Gibbons lasted a full fifteen rounds with the world's heavyweight champion Jack Dempsey without being knocked down made Gibbons a hero with the exuberant crowd. Dempsey, of course, won the fight by a unanimous decision and retained his title.

After the Fourth of July celebration in Shelby, Donnelly and Arnold went to the railroad yard to hop a westbound Great Northern freight train. When the outlaws selected a boxcar and climbed inside, another transient was already riding in the car. The robbers did not want a traveling companion. At gunpoint, they relieved this poor man of what little money he had and kicked him off the train.

The pair of desperadoes arrived back in Bonner County, Idaho,

Dempsey-Gibbons Heavyweight Title Fight at Shelby, Montana on July 4, 1923. The crowds of people at the Jack Dempsey vs. Tommy Gibbons world heavyweight championship boxing match were the perfect cover for Mike Donnelly and Noah Arnold. They could hide in the crowd and spend some of the money taken from the bank in Plains, Montana. (950-443, Montana Historical Society, Helena, Montana)

around July 12. They got off the train north of Sandpoint and went first to a waterhole on the wooded ridges north of Kootenai, in the same area where they'd hid after robbing the Ponderay Hotel. The next day they made their way east to the cabin on Boyer Hill that they had discovered just before going to Plains. This time they stayed in the shack for a few days. It is believed that they buried what was left of the currency from the bank robbery somewhere near the cabin.

30

Murder at Hope, Idaho

THE CRIME SPREE RESUMED on Monday, July 16. The two outlaws left their hideout and walked the Northern Pacific tracks toward Hope, Idaho, about ten miles east. They intended to continue all the way back to Plains, Montana, to retrieve the bag of coins taken in the bank robbery there.

Noah Arnold was wearing a short mackinaw coat. Mike Donnelly was wearing a blue overcoat, and he carried their gear in a packsack on his back. The men walked about a mile and a half to Culver Spur. There, they had to step off the tracks and let Hugh R. Sage, a signal maintainer for the Northern Pacific, pass by in his speeder. Sage was also traveling east toward Hope. As he passed, he noticed the butt of a large pistol in Arnold's hip pocket, and that Arnold was wearing an army cartridge belt. Sage wondered what the men were up to.

A few hours later, the men again met Sage in his motor car, on his way back to Sandpoint.

Late that afternoon, Sage saw the armed strangers a third time as he headed home to Hope at the end of his workday. He had a feeling that these men were up to no good, but he did not notify anyone of his suspicions.

Donnelly and Arnold arrived in Hope after dark. Shortly after ten p.m., they appeared at the front door of William A. Crisp's general store and pool hall. The store, which had pool tables and card tables in the back room, was located in the former Rainier Hotel building, just west of the old Jeannot Hotel. Will Crisp was counting the day's receipts. James Campbell, the Hope postmaster, was in the store visiting with Crisp and waiting for him finish so that they could walk up the hill to their homes together.

Hope, Idaho, in the Summer of 1923. Will Crisp is seen on the porch of his store and pool hall in the center of the photo. (Bonner County Historical Museum)

Arnold tried the door handle, but it was already locked. Crisp went to the door and asked what the men wanted. Arnold said that they wanted to buy a loaf of bread, so Crisp unlocked the door and let them in. When the storeowner turned to get the bread, both Arnold and Donnelly drew handguns and pointed them at Crisp and Campbell. Donnelly told Campbell to turn and face the wall, and held a gun to his back.

Arnold gathered up all the money that he could find and then went through the storeowner's pockets. When Arnold tried to take a gold watch that Will Crisp's father had given him, Crisp cursed and tried to reach the telephone. Arnold cocked his pistol and demanded that Crisp raise his hands higher or he would shoot. A struggle ensued between Crisp and Arnold. Arnold had the muzzle of his pistol poked into the right side of Crisp's abdomen, and the trigger-happy bandit squeezed the trigger. The .45-caliber slug from Arnold's revolver tore through the victim's intestines and bladder and lodged in his left thigh. Crisp sank to his knees, then fell face forward onto the floor. Donnelly tried to shoot the fallen store-keeper in the back with his .32-.20 revolver. The pistol's hammer clicked, but the weapon did not fire.

Campbell watched the scuffle over his shoulder. When he turned to help his wounded friend by grabbing Donnelly's arm, Donnelly hit him over the head with the butt of his disabled pistol, knocking Campbell unconscious. Arnold then shot twice at Camp-bell, now lying on the floor, and narrowly missed. The slugs from Arnold's .45 lodged in the boards of the wooden floor just inches from Campbell's head. The fallen man's scalp started bleeding from the pistol whipping, and the bandits thought they had shot him in the head.

Arnold bent over Crisp and took the keepsake watch from the wounded man's pocket. Then, without checking on Campbell, the bandits fled from the pool hall with the gold watch and more than a hundred dollars in cash and checks. They slid down the high embankment across the street from the store and ran away to the west on the Northern Pacific tracks. They decided to return to their hideout cabin rather than continue on to Montana. They knew that the shooting incident would bring the police out in force.

When James Campbell regained his senses, he managed to tele-phone Dr. N. R. Wallentine in Sandpoint. Then Campbell went to George Badgley's house nearby and awakened him and his fam-ily. Soon half the town of Hope was at the scene, including signal maintainer Hugh Sage. Sage felt terrible that he had not reported his sightings of the suspicious-acting men earlier that day. Perhaps doing so would have saved Will Crisp's life.

The doctor, after notifying the sheriff's office of the emergency call, drove his automobile at once to Hope, arriving there about eleven forty-five p.m. Will Crisp was sitting in a chair. He never lost consciousness, but he was badly hurt. The Crisp family was at the store in their nightclothes, along with the other townspeople who had gathered.

Immediately upon being notified, Bonner County Sheriff William Kirkpatrick organized a posse of Sandpoint men to guard the railroad and highway between Sandpoint and Hope. He also telephoned Clark Fork, Idaho, and the Montana towns of Heron, Noxon, and Thompson Falls, asking authorities to watch for the holdup men there.

The wounded man was placed in the baggage car on the No. 3 Northern Pacific passenger train early Tuesday morning, bound for Sacred Heart Hospital in Spokane. Crisp's wife, Josephine, and her sister Eliza, who was visiting from California, accompanied him.

Will Crisp did not make it. He died about eight a.m. in Spokane.

Doctors did not perform any procedures on the murder victim at the hospital. Crisp's remains were taken to the Alexander Turnbull undertaking parlors at W. 1019 First Avenue in Spokane, where the .45-caliber bullet was removed from the body for evidence and the body was embalmed.

31

Lawmen in Hot Pursuit

LAW ENFORCEMENT OFFICERS in the entire Inland Empire area of eastern Washington, northern Idaho, and western Montana were informed of the shooting and were given descriptions of the perpetrators. About six o'clock on the Tuesday morning after the shooting, Spokane policeman Robert Higginbotham arrested two men who fit the description of Donnelly and Arnold. The two men jumped from a freight train as it rolled into Spokane from Idaho. Officer Higginbotham pursued the suspects to the corner of Trent Avenue and Bernard Street, where he overtook them. With his service revolver drawn, he ordered them to stop and to put their hands up where he could see them. Neither of the men was armed when they were apprehended, but they were found to have a number of .38-caliber pistol cartridges tied up in a bag.

The suspects were booked on open charges until Bonner County Sheriff William Kirkpatrick—accompanied by George Henning, a Hope lumberman, and James Campbell, the Hope postmaster—arrived in Spokane to interview the detainees. The strangers, who said their names were William Monson and James Austin, turned out to be the wrong men. They were released that afternoon.

That same morning, Tuesday, July 17, the two murderers were reported seen in the Trestle Creek area northwest of Hope. Deputy sheriffs organized a posse of men in Sandpoint to follow up on that lead. These lawmen joined with another posse from the Hope and Pack River area. The large combined posse began to "beat the brush" where the suspects were sighted in Cochran's Draw on Trestle Creek. Others searched in the timber between Eagan Mountain and Round Top Mountain. It was raining heavily that day, and by the end of the day, the posse had found no trace of the wanted men.

Through the night, sentries positioned on the highway bridges and railroad bridges at Pack River and Clark Fork remained on guard. The guards on the highway bridge across Pack River, between Hope and Sandpoint, were Jud "Havie" Haviland of Clark Fork, Buster Ellis of Hope, and Alec Gazoff from Oregon, an employee at the Sloan Construction Company. Buster Ellis, who was armed with a revolver, was only fifteen years old. At that time, the Pack River bridge was located against the hills, about a mile north of the present highway bridge.

The weather was unsettled that night, with occasional local thunderstorms. Visibility was very poor. At about two thirty a.m. on Wednesday, July 18, the two fugitives, trying to get back to their hideout on Boyer Hill, attempted to sneak past the three guards on the bridge across Pack River. A heavy, dark cloud hung over the bridge, and the fugitives got very near the guards before they were spotted by Ellis. All three of the startled guards fired their weapons at the same time toward the suspects. The guards did not know it, but one of Gazoff's rifle bullets cut Mike Donnelly across the back of the left wrist, and another guard's bullet creased Donnelly's forehead, stunning him and knocking him down.

The guards heard Noah Arnold roll under the bridge railing and drop about ten feet into the willows growing beneath the bridge. The sentries blindly fired a hail of bullets into the darkness, toward the crashing sound of Arnold running away through the brush. When the guards had used up all of their ammunition, they left their post—unknowingly leaving Donnelly lying wounded on the deck of the bridge.

Donnelly was knocked out for about ten minutes. When he came to, he lay there about half an hour longer before he regained his senses. Then he, too, dropped from the bridge into the willows below just as daylight was breaking. The wounded man swam back to the east side of the river. When he crawled out of the water, he heard someone approaching him through the brush. Donnelly pulled his revolver, thinking it might be a posse man, but Arnold, who could see Donnelly in the twilight, called out, "Mike, Mike, don't shoot. It's me."

The bridge guards informed the sheriff of the incident at the Pack River bridge. A posse formed at the bridge at sunrise, about four a.m. The posse men found a pool of blood on the bridge deck from Donnelly's profusely bleeding scalp wound and realized, for the first time, that one of the fugitives had been wounded. Below the bridge they found Donnelly's canvas packsack, in which they discovered the murder weapon, a .45-caliber Colt revolver. The pack also contained a dark gray cap, a can of coffee, some meat and cheese, and a leather hood with eyeholes, made from the lining of a sheepskin coat.

The trackers found the spot where the fugitive crossed back across the swollen river. From there, a blood trail led the posse more than a hundred yards down the east side of Pack River, where they discovered the wounded man's heavy, wet overcoat abandoned on a boom log.

Sheriff Kirkpatrick brought his bloodhound "Major" to the scene to help follow the suspects, in case the human trackers lost the blood trail. The blood drops led into the woods on the east side of Pack River and up toward Trout Creek. The trail took the posse between the John J. Lloyd and William Anderson ranches. They found where the wounded man had lain down, leaving another pool of blood. The trail ended there. The dog was put on the scent, but he was excited and refused to work.

The posse searched all day Wednesday. The main body of the posse continued to comb the rugged wooded country where the blood trail had led them. They found evidence that someone had camped in the area the night before. The vegetation was matted where men had lain on the ground, and there were remains of food. Guards with binoculars were placed on all hill tops and high points to watch for signs of the wanted men. But by the end of the day, neither of the fugitives was sighted.

Headquarters for the manhunt were established at the home of

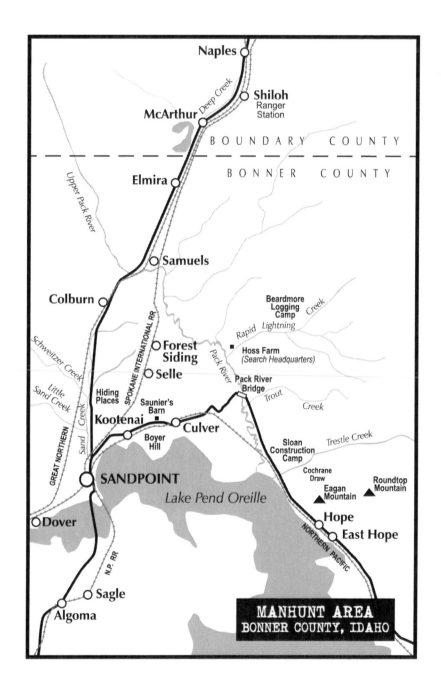

MANHUNT AREA
BONNER COUNTY, IDAHO

Raymond and Daisy Hoss and their five children on Rapid Lightning Creek, a little more than a half mile upstream from where the creek flowed into Pack River. The Charles W. Beardmore Company log flume and logging road went right across the forty-acre tract belonging to the Hoss family. Ray Hoss had a contract with the Beardmore Company to keep the road repaired.

All night long, posse men conducted patrols in the triangle-shaped piece of forest east of Pack River and south of Rapid Lightning Creek, including the ridge between Rapid Lightning Creek and Trout Creek. Guards were posted on all trails, roads, and bridges in the area and on the walkway along the length of Beardmore's elevated flume. Every avenue of escape was thought to be covered. Searchers were rotated in and out in shifts. At the Hoss ranch, meals were served to the posse twenty-four hours a day, and the men took turns sleeping there.

At daybreak (about four thirty a.m.) on Thursday, July 19, County Engineer Charles Tigglebeck, who was guarding along Rapid Lightning Creek at the Beardmore logging camp, spotted the two suspects on the road to the east of him as they came out of the brush and approached the camp. He believed that they were planning to steal food from the camp. Without hesitation, Tigglebeck fired two quick shots at the men as they jumped off the road back into the thick brush. One of the fugitives fired a shot back at Tigglebeck.

Shortly after their encounter with Tigglebeck, the two fugitives made their escape by jumping into the log flume. The flume fell a total of 619 feet in elevation from its head at the logging camp on Flume Creek to Pack River below. The water in the flume was flowing about twenty miles an hour. The men rode the flume four miles, down to Pack River. From there, they waded into Pack River and traveled downstream three more miles before leaving the river and making their way back to their hideout cabin on Boyer Hill. The temperature that day reached eighty-four degrees, so the men were not cold in their wet clothing, which dried quickly anyway.

Back at the hideout cabin, the bandits had cached clothing and other supplies. When they had left the cabin three days earlier, they had been planning to return in a few days to pick up the money hidden there. Now, with all of the trouble that they were in, they decided to bury the gold watch and money from the Crisp pool hall robbery, just as they had done with currency from the Montana bank robbery. They did not want to be captured with evidence that linked them to the murder.

The two men planned to hide in and around the cabin as long as necessary. They had some food with them, and there were wild berries in the nearby woods. They also knew where there was a strawberry patch and vegetable garden that they could raid at night, as long as they were careful not to leave any evidence that they had been there.

Beardmore Lumber Company Log Flume on Rapid Lightning Creek. Baldy Mountain in the distance. (Bonner County Historical Museum)

32

A Frustrating Manhunt

WHILE THE MANHUNT WAS GOING ON, George Palm, a clerk for the Northern Pacific Railroad at the Sandpoint depot, went to Spokane to accompany the return of William Crisp's remains. His body was brought back to Hope in a baggage car on Tuesday, July 17. Palm also brought back the .45-caliber bullet that had been removed from Crisp's body for evidence.

Funeral services were held for Will Crisp on Thursday morning, July 19, at his home in Hope. He was laid to rest in the Hope Cemetery. The funeral was conducted by the Sandpoint Elks Lodge and attended by scores of neighbors and friends. However, practically every man in Hope and many from Sandpoint were absent from the funeral, because were in the hills in the Rapid Lightning Creek and Pack River area, searching for the murdering bandits. The number of men in the posse had grown to nearly 200 loggers, forest rangers, and experienced hunters—all heavily armed. There was little expectation that the fugitives would ever be brought back alive, because feelings among local citizens were running very high against the pair.

By this time, authorities were sure that they were looking for ex-convicts Mike Donnelly and Noah Arnold. Since the men were wanted in Washington for parole violations, bloodhounds were sent to the search area from the Washington State Penitentiary at Walla Walla. Two prison bloodhounds and their handler arrived on the No. 2 Northern Pacific passenger train on the night of Will Crisp's funeral. It was two a.m. on the morning of Friday, July 20, when the hounds and their handler, Prison Guard E. Arthur McNall, arrived at the posse's headquarters at the Hoss ranch.

A report of shooting and screaming near a farmhouse during

the night was received at the command post. At daylight the blood-hounds were taken to investigate. The family at the farmhouse in question was found to be safe, and it appeared to be a false alarm. After conducting his investigation at the farmhouse, an exhausted Sheriff Kirkpatrick, who had been out in the search area for two days and two nights, returned to Sandpoint to get a few hours' rest.

It was not until several hours after daylight on Friday morning that the prison bloodhounds and Sheriff Kirkpatrick's bloodhound were taken to the Pack River highway bridge in an attempt to fol-low the fugitives. The searchers started from there because that was the last positive place the wanted men were known to have been. Donnelly's abandoned blue overcoat was used to give the scent to the dogs, but the dogs could not pick up the trail. The posse did not know that the fugitives had already slipped through the cordon of men placed around the area.

On Thursday night, someone stole butter from a root house and then raided a chicken coop near the town of Naples, Idaho. Later that night, five loaves of bread were taken from the Shiloh Ranger Station north of McArthur. Early Friday morning, July 20, reports were received that a woman saw two men answering the description of the suspects wading in Deep Creek near McArthur.

City Marshal John A. Worley, Night Marshal Ray Lyons, and sheriff's deputies Charles R. Knight (a mail carrier) and Patrick H. Callahan (a local log scaler) were already in the McArthur area, looking for the fugitives. These four lawmen, all from Bonners Fer-ry, had been hunting for the wanted men since the day after the murder. On that Friday, about fifty-five additional Bonner County posse men rushed to McArthur to join these Boundary County of-ficers. A short time later, Boundary County sheriff William Frank Dunning brought thirty more posse men, armed with rifles and pis-tols, from Bonners Ferry to McArthur. A cordon was placed around the search area.

After nothing was found around McArthur, ten Bonner County men stayed with the thirty-four-man Boundary County posse. The joint posse positioned itself just south of Naples to guard the highway and two railroads, which are all close together at that point. The other forty-five Bonner County men returned to the Rapid Lightning Creek/Pack River search area.

Around noon on Friday, a rancher sighted a pair of men in Paradise Valley near Bonners Ferry. These men were on a road that led to Crossport, a station on the Great Northern Railroad east of Bonners Ferry. It was assumed that this was evidence that the wanted men were heading north. Some thought that they might be heading into Canada. The Royal Canadian Mounted Police were notified to be on the lookout at the border for the fugitives.

On Friday afternoon, a large part of the Bonner County posse, the Walla Walla bloodhounds, and Sheriff Kirkpatrick's bloodhound "Major" were pulled from the search area around lower Pack River and sent to the area of the sighting in Boundary County. Again, no trace of the murderers was found.

About eight p.m. on Friday, Len Arnett, a Sandpoint cement contractor, and Rev. Claude B. Martin, minister at the Sandpoint Methodist Church, were standing guard on the side of a hill in the Pack River search area. They spied what they thought was a man sneaking through the timber in the twilight. Adrenaline pumping, the excited guards fired four shots just before their target dodged out of sight.

Based on this sighting by Arnett and Martin, practically all of the posse and the hounds were brought back from Boundary County to the original search area on Saturday morning. The posse was almost frantically racing back and forth between reported sightings in a desperate attempt to catch the murderers. The posse was expending a tremendous amount of time and energy chasing "phantoms."

No human tracks were found at the spot where the sentinels, Len Arnett and Reverend Martin, had seen and shot at a figure as it crossed an opening among the trees, and the bloodhounds could not pick up the scent of the fugitives. But the searchers did find bear tracks, and the trackers routed a small black bear by throwing rocks down the hillside into the brush.

Shortly after noon on Saturday, the entire posse was called in
to meet with Sheriff Kirkpatrick at the Sloan & Hastings road construction camp on Trestle Creek. It was decided at that meeting that
the guards had seen a bear. It was also believed that the men seen
going north near Bonners Ferry were likely the fugitives and that
they had made their escape.

The Washington State Penitentiary bloodhounds were sent
home. Most of the posse men returned to their homes on Saturday
afternoon to bathe, rest, and get a change of clothing. Many men
had been wearing the same clothes for four days. About twenty
posse men remained on duty.

New warnings were issued to cities and towns around the area,
advising people that these two dangerous men were not contained
and could, at this time, be anywhere. As a result of this alarm, new
reports of sightings began coming in, but none of them could be
confirmed as being the fugitives.

On Sunday, July 22, reports were received that two men answering the descriptions of the wanted men were seen at Sinclair,
a flag stop on the Spokane International Railroad. They were seen
again later in the Troy, Montana, train yard, and a third time on
a road across the Kootenai River from Troy, near the Yaak bridge.
The manhunt's focus was immediately transferred to the area of the
Yaak River near Troy.

On Monday, July 23, the sheriff and some twenty to thirty
posse men from Bonner County—including Charlie DeLisle, Jack
Jones, and M. R. Young—were rallied and sent by automobile to
Montana to look for the fugitives. They were joined by Bonners
Ferry City Marshal John A. Worley and three Boundary County
deputies. The Idaho men were operating in Montana under the
sanction of the Lincoln County, Montana, sheriff's office.

Back in Bonner County on Monday, a bloody rag was found
beside the Pack River, and posse men from Sandpoint rushed to the
scene. Their investigation determined that the rag had been left by a
local rancher who had cut his foot while swimming. That same day,
a man was brought to Sandpoint from a railroad construction camp

at Plains, Montana, as a possible suspect. Eyewitness James Campbell said that the man in custody was not one of the men who had robbed and shot Will Crisp on July 16. Patrolman Matt Benson arrested another man on suspicion, but this man was also released when James Campbell again came from Hope to Sandpoint to identify him and declared that he was not one of the wanted men.

Meanwhile, on the Yaak River in Montana, after talking with the people who thought that they had seen the suspects, Sheriff Kirkpatrick decided that the descriptions given were not those of Donnelly and Arnold. While Montana state troopers continued to search for the men seen in Troy just to confirm that they were not the suspects, Sheriff Kirkpatrick and his posse returned to Sandpoint on Tuesday, July 24, and the posse was officially disbanded.

Some posse members continued to search the area northeast of Sandpoint on their own. Trainmen were asked to report any suspicious passengers or "stowaways" to the police. The Bonner County sheriff's office announced that a reward of two hundred and fifty dollars for each man would be paid for information leading to arrests.

33

"Making a Run For It"

WHILE THE CITIZENS OF BONNER and Boundary counties were wearing themselves out chasing elusive fugitive sightings, the real culprits had not moved from their hiding place for six days. Finally the outlaws decided that it was time to leave Bonner County permanently, since they would never be able to move about freely without being recognized. They had no intention of remaining in hiding for the rest of their lives. However, "making a run for it" exposed them to the possibility of detection and capture. They were fairly safe as long as they remained in the remote wooded area where they were hiding, but they would have to take the risk of being seen if they were ever going to escape.

Early Wednesday morning, July 25, the wanted men came out of hiding. They had had no contact with anyone except each other since the day of the shooting, nor had they seen a newspaper since that time. They did not realize that postmaster James Campbell had survived and could identify them. The men were thinking that, with both men shot dead and without physical evidence to link them to the killings, the most that they could be held for, if captured, was parole violation. Therefore, they did not dig up the incriminating stolen money and take it with them. There was always the hope that they could come back later, or send someone, to fetch the money and the gold watch.

The fugitives needed to travel light, so they hid their excess clothing and gear in a pole barn on the Charles F. Saunier ranch, located on the northern edge of the woods where they had been hiding on Boyer Hill. Donnelly also left his pistol in Saunier's barn. He knew that there was a real possibility that they would encounter members of the posse looking for them. Since there were far too many men on the posse to consider risking a shoot-out, as Donnelly would have done in the old days, he felt that things would go easier for him in court if he were unarmed when he was captured. Arnold, however, who had always carried a weapon since he was a teenager, felt safer being armed, and kept a pistol in his pocket.

That Wednesday morning, Donnelly, who was carrying his gear in his packsack, was seen boldly filling a water bottle from Saunier's well. When ranch owner Charles Saunier approached, Donnelly pulled his hat down over the wound on his forehead and put his injured left hand in his pants pocket. Noah Arnold was with Donnelly at the time, but he ducked behind some equipment and remained out of sight.

Saunier asked Donnelly if he was camping in the area. Donnelly acknowledged that he was. Saunier suspected this was one of the wanted men, but he did not want to tip Donnelly off that he was suspicious. The rancher simply asked the suspect to be careful with fire in the woods, and climbed into the seat of his mowing machine to resume work in his hay field. As soon as he was out of sight of Donnelly, Saunier hurried home and telephoned the sheriff.

Saunier's place was on the north side of the state highway to Hope, about two miles northeast of Kootenai. His call sent officers racing to that area, but when the sheriff and about twenty posse men arrived, the outlaws had disappeared. A half mile west of the Saunier ranch, the posse found tracks in the dust where both men crossed the road leading to Selle. They knew that the tracks belonged to the fugitives, because one pair of tracks showed size nine tennis shoes with distinctive holes in the soles.

When Mike Donnelly and Noah Arnold left the Saunier ranch, they fled quickly north together for three and a half miles to Forest Siding on the Spokane International Railroad. At that point the pair split up, agreeing that they would be safer traveling alone because, if captured, they could deny ever having had a partner and could more easily convince authorities that they had nothing to do with the Hope murder. From Forest Siding, Arnold continued walking north on the Spokane International tracks. Donnelly turned south on the tracks toward the community of Selle.

A short time after the fugitives went their separate ways, after walking a mile and a half, Donnelly was spotted by a small boy along the railroad tracks near the Selle "flag stop" station. The boy was frightened and ran home without watching which way the man went. This sighting, telephoned in by the boy's parents, sent five men from Hope and one man from Sandpoint hurrying to Selle in search of the suspect.

Donnelly was aware that the boy saw him, so the fugitive deserted his plan to flee the country. He knew that, by coming out of hiding, there was a risk of being seen, and that is exactly what happened—first by Charles Saunier and now by the boy. Donnelly

Selle Flagstop on the Spokane International Railroad. A young boy reported seeing the fugitive, Mike Donnelly, walking south on these tracks north of Sandpoint through the community of Selle. Donnelly took refuge in the wooded hills in the distance, on the right. (Bonner County Historical Museum)

knew that he had to go back into hiding, because the posse would soon be on his trail.

A mile south of Selle, Donnelly left the railroad tracks and went into those familiar steep, wooded ridges north of Kootenai, where he and Arnold had eluded the police in the past. He found a good place to hide and waited and watched. Donnelly calculated that Arnold, too, would be sighted if he continued running. Donnelly decided not to move. He would let Arnold be a decoy and hopefully distract the posse away from his new hiding place.

34

One Suspect Captured

MIKE DONNELLY'S IDEA of letting Noah Arnold act as a decoy for the posse worked. Wednesday afternoon, about ten miles north of where the outlaw team had split up, a farmer saw Arnold walking north up the Spokane International tracks. The wanted murderer was frightened, sure that the farmer recognized him as one of the fugitives. Arnold continued walking north, but when he was out of the farmer's sight, he ducked over to the Great Northern tracks. The two railroads were only about a hundred yards apart at that point near the Great Northern flag stop depot of McArthur. When Arnold got on the Great Northern tracks, he doubled back and went south toward Sandpoint, about eighteen miles away. Arnold made this maneuver in an attempt to fool the farmer who had seen him walking north on the Spokane International tracks. At this time, Arnold decided to take Donnelly's advice and disarm himself, just in case he was captured. South of McArthur, he stopped and hid his pistol in a pile of rocks.

Arnold's deception did not work. The farmer knew that the man he was watching had changed directions. He telephoned the sheriff's offices in both Bonners Ferry and Sandpoint, reporting that he had seen a man fitting the description of one of the murder suspects going south through McArthur. Following this report, the six-man posse posted at Selle immediately moved their search over to the Great Northern tracks in an attempt to intercept Arnold as he came south. Following the report called in to the Boundary County sheriff's office, deputies Pat Callahan and Earnest E. Saunders (a dry-goods store owner) rushed south from Bonners Ferry to help trap the murder suspect.

About two and a half miles south of where he had been spotted, and with the posse closing in on him, Noah Arnold flagged the No. 43 Great Northern passenger train at the community of Elmira. He calmly boarded the train without arousing the suspicion of Conductor Lewis A. Bruckhauser and bought a ticket to Newport, Washington. The Bonner County posse men arrived at Elmira just ten minutes after the train had gotten underway again, followed shortly by the Bonners Ferry men. One of these lawmen telephoned the sheriff's office in Sandpoint, but the train had left Sandpoint before the sheriff could get some men over to the depot. Sheriff Kirkpatrick then telephoned the Great Northern depot at Priest River, the train's next scheduled stop to the west.

Harry T. Holz, a special railroad agent from Spokane, had been riding freight trains in the area for several days, disguised as a hobo, in the hope of catching the murderers. Agent Holz happened to be in Priest River that afternoon. The Great Northern depot agent at Priest River contacted Holz and arranged for him to board the No. 43 train when it stopped there. Aboard the train, Holz identified himself to Conductor Bruckhauser and told him that a wanted murderer was suspected to be a passenger on his train. When the train left the Priest River station, the special agent immediately took Arnold into custody.

Arnold was removed from the train at Newport, Washington, and turned over to Deputy Sheriff Norman E. Pollack of Pend Oreille County, who took him to the county jail. Neither Pollack nor Holz were absolutely sure that the man they were holding was one of the murderers.

Arnold was searched and found to be unarmed. He had twenty-five cents in his pocket, plus eleven dollars in currency, a check for one hundred dollars, and a pair of rubber gloves sewn into the lining of his coat, in the shoulder just above the sleeve. The check was stolen, but at the time, the police did not know that for sure. Arnold was secretly surprised when he learned from the conversations of the lawmen that only one man, Will Crisp, had died in the Hope shooting incident. Arnold had thought they had left James Campbell dead on the floor as well.

Noah Arnold in the Bonner County Sheriff's Office. Prisoner Noah Arnold was questioned at the sheriff's office in Sandpoint, Idaho, shortly after his capture on July 25, 1923. (Bonner County Historical Museum)

Sheriff Kirkpatrick and several special deputies came from Sandpoint and took the captured man back to the Bonner County jail. At first Arnold told authorities his name was "Robert Ford," the alias he had used for many years. He said that he had been riding a freight train from Essex, Montana, when some fellow riders had thrown him off of the train at Elmira.

The sheriff did not believe his prisoner's story, so on the same afternoon that he was captured, Arnold was taken under heavy guard to a place where a footprint was found on the Great Northern right-of-way at McArthur. A comparison showed that Arnold's shoes with holes in the soles matched the tracks found there.

Arnold admitted to Sheriff Kirkpatrick and the posse men that he had made the tracks earlier in the day when he went into a hay field to ask a farmer the best way to get to Newport. Knowing that it was not the murder weapon, Arnold voluntarily led the officers to the .32-caliber Smith & Wesson revolver that he had hidden under some rocks. He hoped that his honesty and openness would convince authorities that he was innocent and had nothing to hide. Arnold (still using the alias Robert Ford) said that he had hidden the gun a few hours before he was captured. He said that he was a paroled convict from Washington and had violated parole by leaving the state. He explained that he had hidden the pistol because, if picked up and taken into custody, he did not want to be armed, because it would make his parole violation worse. Arnold further claimed to be sneaking around because he was afraid that the posse might mistake him for one of the outlaws who had committed the robbery and murder in Hope and they might shoot him on the spot. The suspect was taken back to jail and locked up in a wire cage within the jail cell, to keep him safe from the other inmates.

35

A "Necktie Party"

ON THURSDAY, JULY 26, a fifty-man posse from the Hope and Pack River area was rallied. The police did not know which man they had captured. Was their prisoner the man seen at Saunier's ranch the day before? Was he the one seen later near the Selle depot? The two men had not been seen together during the previous two days, so maybe only one fugitive had come out of hiding. Sheriff Kirkpatrick decided take to his posse back to Boyer Hill near Saunier's place. The posse men circled Boyer Hill in the hope that Mike Donnelly was still hiding there.

Meanwhile, at the county jail, Noah Arnold was interrogated by Agent Morgan, an operative for the United States Secret Service, who came to Sandpoint from Spokane. Morgan fingerprinted Arnold to positively identify him. It was then that Arnold dropped the alias "Robert Ford." Arnold also admitted that he had participated in the crime that he was being accused of, but blamed Mike Donnelly for the actual killing.

Hope Postmaster James Campbell came to the jail in Sandpoint and positively identified Arnold as the man who had shot William Crisp. When Campbell swore that Arnold fired the round that killed Crisp, Arnold changed his story again and admitted to shooting Crisp, but said that he was "excited" and the gun had gone off accidentally.

In Spokane, Louis A. Bruckhauser, the conductor of the train on which Noah Arnold had been captured, was telling people that he planned to apply to Bonner County for the two-hundred-and-fifty-dollar reward offered for Arnold's capture. Bruckhauser said, "When the man boarded my train, I became suspicious because of his apparent nervousness, and for the reason that he fitted the description of the smaller Hope bandit. I accused him of being one of the fugitives and he seemed frightened. When the train reached Sandpoint, I telephoned to the sheriff's office, and a woman answered and said that all the men of the force were in the country seeking the fugitives. I then telephoned the chief of police, receiving the same information. I wired ahead to Newport and turned the man over to Deputy Sheriff N. E. Pollack, who met the train."

Of course, Special Agent Holz, Deputy Pollack, and others refuted the conductor's story. Louis Bruckhauser did not collect the reward. In fact, there is no evidence that the reward was ever paid to anyone.

When Thursday's search for Donnelly on Boyer Hill produced zero results, Sheriff Kirkpatrick, Deputy Sheriff Pete Schainstine, and a number of posse men—including George Badgley, Leo Mintz, and W. W. Philbrick, all of Hope—dragged Arnold out of jail on Friday. They hauled him to Saunier's ranch, where they ordered him to show them his partner's hiding place or he would be sorry.

Noah Arnold Being Questioned by the Posse. Photograph from the *Northern Idaho News* of August 7, 1923. (Bonner County Historical Museum)

When Arnold began lying about locations, several men pulled him from the sheriff's grasp. They secured his hands behind his back and put a blindfold over his eyes. A noose was placed around his neck, and the other end of the rope was thrown over a pulley-pole on Saunier's barn. When asked if he had any last words before being hanged, the terrified prisoner began singing "Nearer My God to Thee." Posse men pulled on the rope and suspended Arnold in the air for a few seconds. County Physician Dr. Floyd G. Wendle photographed the near-hanging.

Renegade Posse Threatens to Hang Noah Arnold. A group of Bonner County posse men took suspect Noah Arnold and threatened to hang him if he did not tell where his partner was hiding. (Bonner County Historical Museum)

What the newspapers called a "necktie party form of the third degree" was effective. When Arnold was lowered to the ground and given a second chance to talk, he started cooperating. He showed the posse the cache of clothing in Saunier's barn, which also held Donnelly's .32-.20-caliber revolver and a pair of rubber gloves. He then took the posse to the place where he and Donnelly were hiding among the rocks on Boyer Hill on Tuesday night, before they split up. Arnold even showed the posse the shack where he and Donnelly had stayed at times.

Arnold then took them to a rugged area west of the Spokane International Railroad tracks. These wooded ridges were in an area in the middle of a triangle that would be formed by drawing lines between Kootenai, Selle, and Bronx. He showed them various water holes where he and Donnelly had sometimes hid. Arnold did not know it, but Donnelly was actually hiding in these hills at the time. Donnelly was not found at any of the places Arnold showed the posse, but the sheriff believed that they were getting close to the second fugitive.

36

The Trail Grows Cold

AT FIVE O'CLOCK IN THE AFTERNOON, the sheriff put out a call for more men so that a massive manhunt could be mounted in this area of stump ranches and logged-over land north of Kootenai, which had not been searched before. Sheriff Kirkpatrick also sent again for the bloodhounds from the penitentiary at Walla Walla.

The posse that assembled on Friday evening, July 27, was not large enough to surround the cluster of steep, thicketed ridges where the sheriff was sure that Donnelly was hiding. They needed to secure the perimeter of an area about three miles long and two miles wide, bounded by Selle Road on the north, the road to Bonners Ferry on the west, and the Spokane International Railroad on the east and south. At midnight, the sheriff put out a second call for men to help.

Hugh Winder, manager of the Kootenai Motor Company in Coeur d'Alene, drove two volunteers up to Sandpoint in answer to the sheriff's call for help. When Winder returned to Coeur d'Alene, he told people there that Sandpoint looked like "a wild-west town," with everyone carrying revolvers and rifles.

A search of the thickets north of Kootenai on Friday night, July 27, did not yield the wanted man. The bloodhounds from the penitentiary at Walla Walla arrived with their handler, Art McNall, on Saturday morning. Spokane Commissioner of Public Safety Maurice Smith and Spokane Chief of Police Wesley Turner also drove to Sandpoint to offer their assistance in the search for Donnelly.

At noon the dogs were taken to a spot where a man had crossed the Spokane International Railroad tracks near the north end of Boyer Slough. These were the tracks made by Donnelly the previous Wednesday after being seen by the boy in Selle. The dogs did not pick up a trail, and soon they began to suffer from the excessive heat. The temperature that day was ninety-two degrees and seventy-three percent humidity. The manhunt was halted for a while to give both men and animals a rest.

When it was reported that a shot was fired near the Isaac "Ike" Miller barn, a half mile east of the footprints on the railroad grade, the posse hurried to the vicinity of the shot but discovered nothing. A few posse men were stationed at guard positions in the area around Miller's place, while the main posse returned to the hills north of Kootenai. The searchers finally found the spring where Donnelly had been hiding Wednesday, Thursday, and Friday nights, but he was no longer there.

The sky became cloudy and it cooled down a little. At six o'clock Saturday evening, the dogs were taken to the place where there was evidence that Donnelly had been hiding. The bloodhounds picked up the scent, but soon lost it, as they usually did. Authorities decided that Donnelly must have been putting something on his shoes to throw the dogs off. Of course Donnelly had learned the trick of using ground red pepper early in his career as a fugitive in western Washington. Sheriff Kirkpatrick's hopes had been high. When this latest attempt to capture Donnelly failed, the discouraged sheriff sent the entire posse home.

Back at the sheriff's office, Arnold continued to tell stories about what he knew. Arnold said that, while he was the one who had shot Will Crisp, Donnelly was to blame for everything.

"I was practically his slave as he made me do anything that he wanted me to. This man invited me to go to Crisp's store to buy some bread to make sandwiches. We had hardly stepped into the store before my companion pulled a gun and told Crisp to put up his hands. That was the first that I knew a holdup was to be pulled off," claimed Arnold.

He told authorities that his companion had secretly hidden the gold watch and chain and the checks stolen from Crisp, with the intention of keeping the loot for himself. Arnold also claimed that he did not rob the Ponderay Hotel. He said that he had heard about Donnelly and another man doing that. But since Arnold had not worn a disguise, the hotel night clerk, James Hewett, could identify him as the holdup man.

Arnold could not very well lie about robbing the Plains, Montana, bank since he did not use a mask in that robbery, either. Sheriff P. A. Heater of Sanders County was already in Bonner County, helping the Bonner County posse. He was able to identify Arnold. Arnold admitted that he had robbed the bank in Plains, but that it was another man whose name he did not know (not Mike Donnelly) who had helped him with that robbery. Arnold told Sheriff Kirkpatrick that the thirteen hundred dollars taken in the Plains bank robbery was hidden in Montana, but it was more likely buried near their hideout cabin. There is no indication that the sheriff or anyone else ever found the buried money. Arnold also confessed that he "and others" had robbed many places in small towns in northern Idaho and western Montana during the previous couple of months.

The authorities did not believe the story about a third man or any "other men." A detective from the William J. Burns International Detective Agency, who had been hired by the insurance company for the bank in Plains, came to Sandpoint with Sheriff Heater. This Burns detective felt that all of the evidence pointed solely to Noah Arnold and Mike Donnelly as suspects in the crime spree which had taken place in the region, starting at the end of May.

37

Second Suspect Captured

AT THIS TIME, OUT IN THE SEARCH AREA, Mike Donnelly was just one step ahead of the posse. On Saturday, July 28, while the lawmen were scouring the hills where Donnelly was hiding, he was able to use his skills as a woodsman to avoid the searchers and escape into the area west of Sand Creek. He admitted later, however, that the hounds came very near to him, and he was worried for awhile that he would be captured.

Donnelly went to the Great Northern Railroad tracks between Schweitzer Creek and Little Sand Creek and walked about six miles down the tracks to Dover, skirting Sandpoint on its west edge. The next morning he continued to cautiously sneak west and south down the Pend Oreille River, trying to make it back to the state of Washington.

In the twilight, about eight o'clock on Sunday evening, July 29, Donnelly was seen by Clarence Brown, a signal maintainer for the Great Northern Railroad. Donnelly was headed west through Laclede, eight miles east of Priest River. Brown notified the Great Northern telegraph operator at the Priest River depot, who in turn notified Priest River town marshal, Frank Pleas.

Marshal Pleas stationed guards on the wagon bridge across the Priest River, about a half mile east of the town of Priest River. The marshal and three other men—Dave Berglund, George Binkley, and Bert Fry—lay in wait for Donnelly along the Great Northern tracks near the railroad bridge spanning the same river. These two bridges were only about three hundred fifty yards apart. It was a clear night with an almost-full moon, so visibility was good.

About eleven thirty p.m., the shadowy form of Mike Donnelly was seen approaching the train bridge in the moonlight. Donnelly crept slowly across the bridge, stopping frequently to listen intently to the night sounds and to study carefully the shadows in the moonlight. It took him twenty minutes to completely cross the short trestle on his hands and knees.

When Donnelly reached solid ground, he stood up. He was allowed to walk right past two of the waiting men, whom he could not see in the dark. These two men closed in behind Donnelly as Marshal Pleas and the fourth man confronted him and told him to put his hands up. The fugitive saw that he was surrounded. He immediately placed his hands into the air and surrendered peaceably to the marshal.

Donnelly was unarmed when captured, except for a straight razor that was found in his pocket. A further search of his pockets yielded some keys and a large leather wallet. The contents of the wallet—an I.W.W. union card, twenty-six dollars in bills, and some small change—were water-stained from the four-mile "ride" in the Beardmore log flume a few days earlier. Donnelly was also carrying a packsack containing bacon and a can in which he boiled coffee. The captured fugitive was weak and tired.

Donnelly was taken to the Priest River village jail, where Bert Fry and Dave Berglund, both armed with rifles, stood outside his cell as guards. The Priest River police notified Sheriff Kirkpatrick in Sandpoint of the capture. Priest River physician Dr. Carl P. Getzlaff was summoned to the jail to examine and dress Donnelly's wounds, which were both infected. The wound on the back of his hand was seriously infected and gangrenous.

Donnelly talked freely with his captors while waiting for the county sheriff to arrive, frequently smiling and laughing. He seemed relieved to be in custody. Sheriff Kirkpatrick arrived around two twenty a.m. Monday morning. As the sheriff was taking Donnelly away, the prisoner thanked Dr. Getzlaff for attending to his wounds and assured the Priest River police that he was not angry with them for capturing him. He wished Marshal Pleas a long and happy life.

Donnelly was taken to the county jail in Sandpoint, where Dr. Floyd G. Wendle, county physician, further treated his wounds.

Donnelly continued to laugh and joke with his captors as if it were all some kind of game. For a man who did not like to be locked up, who liked camping in the wide open spaces, and who tried to escape from imprisonment at every opportunity, Donnelly had squandered his freedom. From the time that he was paroled from the Washington State Penitentiary until the time he was back in jail, only seventy-five days elapsed—and very eventful days they were!

Donnelly first told authorities that his name was "Bert Clay" and that he had received his injuries in a brawl in Kingsgate, Brit-

Suspect Mike Donnelly in the Bonner County Jail. When Donnelly was captured on July 29, 1923, both of his gunshot wounds were infected, the one on the back of his hand badly infected. (Bonner County Historical Museum)

ish Columbia, a few days earlier. But Walla Walla Prison Guard Art McNall, in town with the penitentiary's bloodhounds, identified Donnelly as a paroled prisoner from the Washington State Penitentiary. McNall had seen Donnelly at the prison. Also, just by coincidence, C. D. Hansen, a special railroad detective for the Spokane International, was also a former guard at the penitentiary in Walla Walla, and he could identify both Arnold and Donnelly as former inmates at that prison.

Donnelly then admitted his correct name, but he denied involvement in the murder of Will Crisp. He said that he was sneaking across the bridge because he was in violation of his parole in Washington and did not want to go back to prison. Finally, after intense interrogation, Donnelly admitted that he had been involved in the holdup of Crisp's store in Hope, but claimed that he was a lookout outside the store and that a third man named "Benjamin" was inside the store. However, when Hope postmaster James Campbell arrived at the county jail, he positively identified Donnelly as the man who had held him at gunpoint inside the store while Crisp was shot.

After Donnelly's capture, Mrs. Crisp arrived at the Bonner County Jail in an attempt to recover the money stolen from her late husband's store. She was allowed to confront Donnelly, but he only told her that the checks were burned and the currency was gone. This contradicted Arnold's testimony that Donnelly had secretly buried the money and the checks, along with the gold watch.

38

Can There Be a Fair Trial?

EMOTIONS IN THE COMMUNITY were running high against the murderers. Some men from Hope took the steamboat *Henrietta* across Lake Pend Oreille from Hope to Sandpoint, intending to snatch the prisoners out of jail and lynch them.

The Hope men docked the steamboat at the Sandpoint City Dock and sent one of their men up from the waterfront to look over the situation at the county jail on South First Avenue, a quarter of a mile away.

The steamboat *Henrietta* on Lake Pend Oreille Near Hope, Idaho. Vigilantes from Hope steamed up to Sandpoint in the *Henrietta*, intending to snatch the murder suspects from the jail and lynch them. (Bonner County Historical Museum)

City Docks at Sandpoint, Idaho, on Lake Pend Oreille. On Monday, July 30, 1923, a group of angry citizens from Hope, Idaho, moored the steamboat *Henrietta* at the Sandpoint City Dock. They intended to take the punishment of the murder suspects into their own hands. (Bonner County Historical Society Museum)

Law enforcement officers had been tipped off to a potential lynching attempt and were ready for such a possibility, although most officials felt that the chances of it happening were remote. The scout for the vigilantes from Hope returned to the boat and reported that the jail was on high alert. The vigilantes decided that their plan to take the law into their own hands was too risky and called it off.

Because of the lynching rumors, the prisoners were secretly taken to the Kootenai County jail in Coeur d'Alene, fifty miles south of Sandpoint, for safekeeping. On Monday night, July 30, each prisoner was chained to a federal officer and transported in a separate automobile under heavy guard. Each was then placed in a separate jail cell, and Bonner County Deputy Pete Schainstine remained in Coeur d'Alene as a special guard.

From the Coeur d'Alene jail, Donnelly wrote a letter to a man named "G. L. Moore" in Great Falls, Montana. Authorities read the letter. One cryptic sentence, "You know what to do," started the police wondering. Both Donnelly and Arnold had spoken of a third man being involved in their crime spree, though no one really believed them. Now the police wondered, "Could Moore be the third man?"

Sheriff William Kirkpatrick traveled to Great Falls to find Moore and to check him out. Without help from the Great Falls police, Sheriff Kirkpatrick located George L. Moore, who turned out to be another paroled ex-convict from the Washington State Penitentiary. He had been serving a life term for murder at the same time Donnelly was in the penitentiary. They had both worked in the prison jute mill.

Sheriff Kirkpatrick asked for help from law enforcement in Montana. The investigation proved that Moore had had nothing to do with the crimes that Donnelly and Arnold had committed, and authorities in Idaho were still convinced that there was not a "third party" to be considered in their investigation. However, Great Falls authorities were pleased that Kirkpatrick had apprehended Moore, because he had been identified as a man wanted for a recent murder in St. Louis, Missouri.

Donnelly and Arnold were scheduled to be arraigned on Saturday, August 4. The time and place for the arraignment was not announced in advance to avoid attracting a large crowd to the courtroom. The prisoners were brought to Sandpoint from Coeur d'Alene on Friday night, August 3 and arraigned in probate court at ten a.m., Saturday morning, with Judge Myrvin Davis presiding.

Prosecuting Attorney Allen P. Asher told the court that the two defendants were being jointly charged with the crime of first-degree murder. Judge Davis explained to the prisoners that they had the right to counsel, but that if they wanted court-appointed attorneys, they would have to wait until their trial was called in district court. The probate court had no authority to appoint public defenders for them. When asked how they wanted to plead to the charges, both of the accused said, "Not guilty." Judge Davis then scheduled a preliminary hearing for Tuesday afternoon.

The preliminary hearing was held in the probate court on Tuesday afternoon, August 7, at two p.m. Authorities again tried to hold the hearing without attracting public attention, but the word leaked out. Early in the afternoon, people began flocking into the courtroom, which was filled by two o'clock. The crowd overflowed into the court enclosure and the hallway. The suspects were brought into the courtroom, handcuffed together and guarded by four deputies—Edwin Doust, Pete Schainstine, Ray Jagger, and W. J. Geary. Once inside the courtroom, Deputy Doust unlocked the handcuffs.

Mike Donnelly was steady as a rock. He answered distinctly when Probate Judge Myrvin Davis asked him the standard questions. Noah Arnold seemed more ill at ease and mumbled his answers, but he was also fairly steady considering the circumstances.

The prosecutor called three witnesses: the Hope postmaster, James Campbell; Will Crisp's widow, Josephine Crisp; and signal maintainer Hugh R. Sage. Neither defendant took the stand. At the conclusion of the hearing, Judge Davis found probable cause to have both suspects bound over for superior court. He ordered the prisoners held without bond in the Bonner County jail until the scheduled date of their next appearance in court. He explained that, since the offense with which they were charged could possibly bring the death penalty, the defendants were not eligible for bail. Their case was scheduled to be first on the docket of the regular fall term of the district court and slated for a jury trial. Deputy Doust replaced the handcuffs, and the men were led back to the jail.

Back at the jail, Donnelly said matter-of-factly to Sheriff Kirkpatrick, "I intend to escape at the first opportunity."

Because of this threat, security at the jail was tightened. Each prisoner had a separate cell. Neither was ever let out of his cell for any reason. Their meals were pushed to them through the bars. No visitors were allowed in to see them.

Both of Noah Arnold's parents had died during the five years that he was locked up in the penitentiary in Walla Walla, but he still had a number of living brothers and sisters. He wrote a letter from the Bonner County jail to his brother Clayton Arnold in Berea,

Kentucky, just seven miles southeast of where the boys had been raised. In the letter, Noah explained his situation to his brother. He received a reply, so at least some of the family in Kentucky was aware of where he was and what was happening to him.

Bonner County Courthouse at Sandpoint, Idaho. After their arraignment, Noah Arnold and Mike Donnelly were held in the jail in this building until their murder trial on Friday, September 14, 1923. (Bonner County Historical Museum)

39

The Killers Plead Guilty

ON MONDAY, SEPTEMBER 10, 1923, the two defendants were brought before the Eighth Judicial District Court in Sandpoint, with Judge William F. McNaughton of Coeur d'Alene presiding. The defendants were formally charged with murder in the first degree. Both had requested court-appointed attorneys. Sandpoint attorney A. T. Aronson was appointed to defend Noah Arnold. Sandpoint attorney Oscar J. Bandelin was appointed to defend Mike Donnelly. The defendants were given until Wednesday, September 12, to enter pleas.

On September 12, two large bouquets of flowers arrived at the county jail, one for each man. There was no note saying who had sent the flowers and Sheriff Kirkpatrick refused to allow them to be delivered to the prisoners.

Upon the advice of counsel, both men entered pleas of guilty to the charge of first-degree murder. It was the attorneys' understanding that, while the death penalty was allowed by law for first-degree murder, it could only be imposed at the discretion of a convicting jury and could not be inflicted by a judge. It was thought that without a jury trial there could be no death penalty for either man. After the guilty pleas were entered, the panel of jurors was dismissed, but Judge McNaughton said that he still wanted to hear evidence in the case on Friday, September 14.

That Friday, the judge listened to the testimony of the prosecution witnesses. Mike Donnelly's attorney, O. J. Bandelin, sat passively and said nothing in Donnelly's defense. On the other hand, Noah Arnold's attorney, A. T. Aronson, objected to some of the testimony as inadmissible or irrelevant, but the judge overruled all of his objections. Aronson also cross-examined witnesses in an attempt to show his client in a better light. After hearing testimony and examining the evidence, Judge McNaughton said that he would sentence the defendants the following day.

On Saturday, September 15, the courtroom was crowded beyond capacity and the corridors filled with curious onlookers. Many of the spectators were women. When the defendants appeared in court for sentencing, they were both wearing new clothes. Arnold wore a gray sweater with a matching cap, while Donnelly wore a nice blue serge suit. When asked if they had anything to say before sentencing, both men answered that they did not.

Both defendants looked at the judge and listened intently as the sentences were read. Mike Donnelly was sentenced to hard labor in the state penitentiary for the rest of his natural life. Noah Arnold was sentenced to death by hanging. Upon hearing his sentence, Donnelly smiled faintly. Arnold showed no emotion when his sentence was read. Attorney Aronson was shocked by the sentence that his client received and moved for withdrawal of his client's guilty plea. The motion was denied.

The judge ordered the people in the courtroom to remain seated until the prisoners were removed. Officers cleared the aisle and the corridors. The convicts were handcuffed together and led back to the jail, then the spectators were allowed to leave.

At the jail office Arnold spoke his first words, muttering, "I don't give a damn." Then, after being locked in his jail cell, Arnold wildly cursed the court that had condemned him to death. He threatened that, if he ever got out, he would come back to Bonner County and kill some people.

Officials felt that there was a remote possibility that certain Hope citizens, who wanted the death penalty for both men, would try again to exact some form of vigilante justice. No time was lost getting the convicted men out of town on a train. The convicts returned to the county jail from the courtroom at three fifteen p.m. Forty-five minutes later, at four p.m., they were taken aboard a Northern Pacific passenger train handcuffed to Sheriff William Kirkpatrick and Deputy Edwin Doust. The two Bonner County officers accompanied the prisoners to Spokane, where they were turned over to a traveling guard from the Idaho State Penitentiary. The guard took both men to the penitentiary, two miles east of Boise, outside the city limits. When they arrived at the prison on Monday, September 17, Arnold was placed in a death cell.

Entrance to the Grounds of the Idaho State Penitentiary at Boise, Idaho. This is as the entrance appeared when Noah Arnold and Mike Donnelly arrived there on September 17, 1923, as convicted murderers.
(Idaho State Historical Society, Boise, Idaho)

40

A Murderer is Hanged

NOAH ARNOLD WAS SCHEDULED to be hanged on Thursday, November 1, 1923. However, he was granted a reprieve by executive order on the day before the scheduled execution. His attorney, A.T. Aronson, and a new attorney, William M. Morgan of Boise, filed an appeal of his sentence based upon the way that his confession had been handled. Attorney Morgan, who had served as a justice on the Idaho Supreme Court from 1915 to 1920, was hired to defend Arnold by a convict aid society in Boise.

It was cited on appeal that Arnold's defense attorney sought to withdraw the plea of guilty, but was not allowed to do so by the judge. The defense attorneys filed for a new trial because Arnold's confession had been gained, in part, by mob violence. The attorneys claimed that Arnold had been "strung up" in an effort to make him confess. The prosecution, however, maintained that the threatened lynching was not used to extort a confession from Arnold, as he had already confessed to the crime before that incident had taken place. They claimed that the posse was just looking for more information when they threatened to hang their prisoner.

The appeal went all the way to the Idaho Supreme Court. On Saturday, August 9, 1924, the appeal was heard and the sentence of the Eighth Judicial District Court in Sandpoint was upheld by a four-to-one majority of the five justices on the high court. In a majority opinion, Chief Justice Charles P. McCarthy wrote, "The evidence in the record showed a malicious killing while in the act of a felony; that the defendant's rights had not been prejudiced, and that he had been properly warned in court of the consequences of his plea; that the discretion of the court was not abused in pronouncing the extreme penalty." Justice William A. Lee dissented but did not write a dissenting opinion.

Arnold sought a second hearing before the Idaho Supreme Court, but his second appeal was denied. On Monday, October 27, 1924, he was returned to Sandpoint at ten a.m. on the No. 48 Northern Pacific passenger train, accompanied by guards from the penitentiary. At 11:30 a.m., District Judge W. F. McNaughton set a new date for Arnold's execution. He was scheduled to be hanged on December 19. Arnold and his guards left Sandpoint on the train at three ten p.m. that same day.

When Arnold returned to the state penitentiary in Boise, a new plea was filed on his behalf requesting a commutation of his sentence to life imprisonment. The petition asked for a hearing of the case at the pardon board's regular meeting in January 1925. Since members of the pardon board were not in Boise at that time, no action was taken on the petition.

Arnold even wrote a letter to Charlie Young in Pocatello, Idaho, on November 17, asking for help from the National Association for the Advancement of Colored People. But there was nothing that the NAACP could do to stop his execution. The yearlong battle to save Noah Arnold from the gallows failed.

On Wednesday, December 17, Arnold asked to see a minister. Reverend W. B. Williams, a Methodist pastor, came to the prison to talk with Arnold in his death cell. To show his appreciation for the visit, Arnold assigned all of his worldly fortune—thirteen dollars and ninety-nine cents—to Reverend Williams.

The next day, on the eve of his execution, Arnold shook hands with the guards on the day watch and said his good-byes. That night, Guard J. G. Root was assigned to Arnold as his deathwatch. Arnold talked to Root, confessing that he had killed five men during his lifetime. But Arnold insisted that Will Crisp was not one of his victims. He continued to swear that Mike Donnelly had fired the shot that killed Crisp.

Arnold fell asleep about seven p.m. He was awakened from a sound sleep at about eleven forty-five p.m. and informed that he would be executed shortly after midnight. Arnold sighed that he was glad the time had come. He asked to be allowed to change from his prison uniform into his best suit of clothes and that request was granted.

Arnold's arms were strapped tightly to his sides and he was taken to a little anteroom where Warden John Snook read the death warrant to him. Reverend Williams was also in the room, along with guards and a few newspaper reporters.

The condemned man was led out of the little room and across the prison yard to a dimly lighted scaffold in the garden in the northeast corner of the prison yard. This temporary gallows had been built originally for the execution of David Hoagland, who was sentenced to death for the murder of his landlord, William D. Patterson, a Valley County rancher. A last-minute reprieve from the State Board of Pardons had saved Hoagland, who had been seeking a retrial based on new evidence of insanity. The gallows was left standing for the execution of Arnold.

Arnold bravely ascended the gallows steps, standing tall with his shoulders thrown back. Reverend Williams accompanied him up the stairs. It was extremely cold outside. Temperatures reached almost five degrees below zero that night, but Arnold was not shivering. A prison official put a black hood over his head and adjusted the noose around his neck.

An automatic water device was installed on the gallows to release the trap door, so that no individual would need to bear the emotional burden of actually executing the convicted murder. When Arnold stepped back onto the trap door, his weight was supposed to open a faucet on a hose coming from a suspended bucket of water, allowing the bucket to drain. When the bucket was full of water, it counterbalanced a weight on the trap. As the bucket emptied, it would release the weight, which, in turn, would spring the trap door. However, the water in the hose was frozen and the device did not work. The guards worked feverishly to thaw the hose with hot water. Finally there was the sound of water trickling out of the bucket.

The trap was sprung at 12:18 a.m. Noah Arnold was pronounced dead at 12:27 a.m. on Friday, December 19, 1924. His execution was the first hanging in Idaho since May 7, 1909, when Fred Seward was hanged for killing his estranged girlfriend, Mrs. Clara O'Neil, in Moscow, Idaho. None of Noah Arnold's family in Kentucky claimed his body, and he was buried in the prison cemetery.

Part IV

THE LAST HALF OF DONNELLY'S LIFE

41

Desperate Attempts to Escape

ON SEPTEMBER 17, 1923, after fewer than eleven weeks on the outside since his release from the Washington State Penitentiary, Mike Donnelly found himself back in prison at the Idaho State Penitentiary, where he was designated as Inmate 3302. But Donnelly loudly vowed that he would not be in prison long. He told everyone, including Warden W. L. Cuddy, that he would escape someday.

Conditions at the Idaho State Penitentiary were at an all-time low when Donnelly arrived. There were approximately three hundred prisoners housed in only one hundred sixty antiquated jail cells, two men per cell. Much of the cell equipment dated back to the old territorial prison days. With no running water or toilet facilities inside the prison, the very unsanitary "bucket system" of removing and disposing of body waste was used.

The penitentiary had a number of places to work. About eighty prisoners were employed at keeping the prison running smoothly from day to day. Cooks, waiters, dish washers, bakery workers, and helpers worked in the kitchen and dining room. Elsewhere in the prison, there were janitors, laundry workers, hospital workers, clerks, and groundskeepers. A shoe shop employed fifteen prisoners. A barbershop, a tailor shop, and a library employed a few skilled men. A few more skilled clerical workers helped out in the offices of the warden and the captain of the guards.

Twenty-five to thirty men worked under armed guard on the Eagle Island farm, the prison's dairy, where about thirty cows were milked every day. There was also a poultry ranch where both chickens and turkeys were raised.

The largest work site, however, was a shirt factory, which employed about half of the prison population. The factory had been constructed not long before Mike Donnelly arrived at the penitentiary. The workers at this factory made heavy-duty work shirts. Reliance Manufacturing Company, a large shirt company, furnished the raw materials needed at the factory and then purchased the finished products. Prison officials hoped to use profits made at the shirt factory to build a new dormitory for young, first-time offenders. Donnelly was placed on a job at this shirt factory, where inmates labored under the watchful eye of armed guards in cages.

Prisoners at the shirt factory started work at about eight a.m. and worked almost eight hours per day, five and a half days a week. The evening meal was served at four thirty p.m., and the prisoners were locked in their cells shortly after eating. The guards changed shifts at six p.m., and all prisoners were checked and accounted for at every changing of the guards. "Lights out" was at nine thirty p.m. Prisoners were locked in their cells all night until after the changing of the guards at six a.m. Everything was very routine and predictable.

Donnelly was not just bragging when he said that he would try to break out. After getting acquainted in the prison, he did some trading with his fellow inmates to obtain possession of a hacksaw blade which had been smuggled into the prison earlier.

During the times that he was not supervised, Donnelly quietly and patiently went to work. He sawed the hinges on his old cell door until each hinge was near the breaking point. Guards did not notice the fine cuts because the hinges still held the door in place and the door opened and closed normally. The sawing project was completed about three months after Donnelly arrived at the prison.

On Tuesday, December 11, 1923, the convicted murderer was ready to make his break. After "lights out," when most everyone was sleeping, Donnelly quietly finished sawing through the hinges. The powerful man gently set the heavy wooden cell door aside. He quietly made his way down the dimly lighted corridors and out of the cellblock into the main prison yard, where he was confronted by a night guard. Donnelly knew that, at night, only the guards on the wall were armed. Big Mike Donnelly threatened the smaller guard with the hacksaw blade, and the guard backed off. Donnelly then sprinted across the lighted exercise yard to the outside wall.

Guards in the towers on the wall spotted the escaping prisoner. Sirens sounded and spotlights glared, but Donnelly continued running. Commands to halt were given, but Donnelly did not heed them. Before he could make it to the outside wall, a shot rang out and a bullet from the .30-.30-caliber rifle of Prison Guard William Larter hit him in the arm and shoulder. He went down and was quickly subdued.

Idaho Governor Charles C. Moore later commended Larter for shooting the escaping prisoner. When five prisoners embarrassed prison officials by cleanly escaping from the penitentiary in June 1923, Governor Moore provided all of the prison guards on the wall with brand new .30-.30 rifles. He gave the order for guards to do whatever was necessary to prevent a man from escaping, which included shooting to kill.

The wounded convict was taken to the prison hospital, housed in a little old stone building that had once been a blacksmith shop and a carpenter shop. After his stay in the hospital, Donnelly was transferred to solitary confinement in a cellblock for unruly prisoners located next door to the hospital in the southeast corner of the prison complex. He was placed on a diet of bread and water for punishment.

The solitary confinement building was new, built earlier in 1923. It was a low, gray, concrete structure, about eight feet high and twenty-six to twenty-seven feet square. A single door with heavy locks provided the only access to the building. Inside, the small, dark space was partitioned into six cells. Each of the cells had its own two-hundred-pound door with a heavy lock. It was thought that there was no chance to escape from this "dungeon."

Each cell had a round hole, three inches in diameter, in the ceiling for ventilation. These vents, which were open to the elements outside, allowed a tiny bit of light into the cell, but also allowed the cold air, rain, and snow to filter into the unheated cells.

Several inmates were crowded into each tiny cell, depending on the number of men being punished at any given time. Each inmate was issued a blanket. There were beds with steel frames and wire springs in the cells, but often there were not enough beds to go around. The "bucket method" of sanitation was used here, as in the rest of the prison.

Six months in solitary was usually more than enough time to make even the most unruly convict mellow and submissive. Of all the harsh conditions in the dungeon, the continuous darkness seemed to be the hardest to endure. Inmates referred to the place as the "bughouse." Too much time in solitary could make a man "stir crazy."

After his release from solitary confinement, Donnelly returned to his job at the shirt factory, but he continued to be unruly and uncooperative. As a result, he was placed back into the dungeon. With sixteen unruly prisoners crowded into six small cells, conditions were unbearable.

Inside the solitary confinement building, Donnelly became the ringleader of ten other hardened criminals, many of whom had a history of escape and attempted escape. Together these desperate men began making plans for a nearly impossible breakout.

On Monday, August 2, 1926, work on the escape plan started. The six other, less hardened, inmates living in solitary confinement were forced to go along with the insane scheme that Donnelly and his gang concocted.

The prisoners worked through the night. Some tore up blankets and twisted them into ropes from which they made a ladder. A grappling hook for scaling the wall was made with bent iron pipe from a metal bed frame. Others began taking off cell doors. Locks were cut off of individual cell doors with files and hacksaw blades that had been smuggled into the dungeon. The two hundred-pound steel doors were lifted from their hinges so that the escapees would have a clear path to freedom. When they rushed the guards, a door could not be slammed in their faces.

The plan was to overpower the guards who came to check on

the prisoners in the dungeon each morning. It is not clear how these foolhardy men planned to get outside the main prison, but it was believed that part of the plan was to hijack one of the prison trucks and drive away.

At about eight o'clock Tuesday morning, as the guards approached the solitary confinement building to make their regular rounds of inspection, Captain of the Guards Myron Lester heard unusual noises coming from inside the cell block. The inmates had not finished their preparations in time!

Captain Lester ordered the guards on the wall to train their rifles on the entrance to the dungeon, and he summoned Deputy Warden D. W. Ackley. When everyone was in position, the door to the maximum-security facility was flung open by guards who quickly stepped aside, leaving the door to the prison yard unobstructed. The puzzled inmates cautiously approached the opening and peered outside. When the gang leaders saw the battery of rifles pointed at the narrow doorway, they knew that their plan had failed and they did not go any farther. To keep up a brave front, the inmates started shouting and jeering and bragging about how they had trashed the facility.

On Monday, August 9, construction was started on a new solitary confinement building while the old building was repaired. While work was being completed on the new facility, the warden was forced to temporarily house the sixteen incorrigible prisoners in regular prison cells.

During this time, Donnelly apparently had a change of heart. Finally, it appeared that the defiant prisoner had accepted submission to authority. He began to cooperate fully with the prison staff and was back to his old good-natured, likeable self.

In his spare time, Donnelly liked to read, and his reading ability improved well beyond the level that it had been when he left school at age thirteen. He particularly enjoyed reading Hindu and Chinese philosophy. And, believe it or not, Mike Donnelly was a bit of an artist, skilled at hand-painting decorative greeting cards.

After a little more than a year, Donnelly's behavior prompted the new warden, Joseph W. Wheeler, to deduct what was called the "good time allowance" from his sentence. This time off for good behavior was a standard reward, offered in the hope that it would encourage prisoners to do well and to not cause trouble.

However, in spite of the fact that he was friendly, cooperative, and never violent or belligerent, Donnelly's attitude about staying in prison had not changed. He was a patient man, but he had no intention of remaining locked up for the rest of his life. He was always thinking about ways to escape.

Donnelly was returned to his job at the prison shirt factory with a group of potentially dangerous prisoners, who all worked under the watchful eyes and rifle muzzles of heavily armed guards. Donnelly befriended several of these hardened criminals working with him, including another man convicted of murder. Together Donnelly and six other inmates hatched a daring plot. Less than two years after his last escape attempt, and with a new warden who trusted him and had commended his behavior, it was time for Donnelly to move on this latest jailbreak plan.

A prison truck regularly backed up to the doors of the shirt factory shipping room where Donnelly and the other men worked. Inmate laborers loaded the truck with finished shirts for delivery on the outside. The conspirators arranged to have weapons smuggled to them from the outside. The plan was that, on the day chosen for the break, Donnelly would give a signal and the armed convicts would storm the truck while it was being loaded. They would seize one of the guards and use him as a shield while they hijacked the truck from the driver. The escapees would only need to drive the truck thirty feet before passing behind another building, which would shield them from the gunfire of the guards. They would need to race the truck two hundred feet farther to the flimsy main gate of the prison, which could be easily crashed by a speeding truck. There were usually only two guards stationed near the gate, and these guards would not be able to prevent the escape.

The plan would have worked if it had been kept a complete surprise. However, that element of surprise was missing. During the first week of July 1928, prison officials were tipped off by other convicts. The prisoners implicated in the escape plot were put under surveillance and officials knew when they were about to make their move.

Just before the escape was to take place, Warden Joe Wheeler ordered the suspected prisoners seized and searched for weapons. When all of the men were found to be armed, they were thrown into solitary confinement.

Warden Wheeler said, "Out of all the prisoners in the penitentiary, no more dangerous crowd could have gotten together than the seven men who were in on this plot."

42

Five Years in "Siberia"

THE WARDEN HAD ABSOLUTE CONTROL over who was put into the "dungeon" and how long they would stay there. Warden Wheeler, who had trusted Donnelly, was of a mind to put him in this dark hole and throw away the key. Donnelly was branded "the most dangerous prisoner at the Idaho State Penitentiary" and was thought to have no hope for rehabilitation.

Things had changed in solitary confinement since the last time Donnelly had been housed there. As a direct result of the destruction caused by Donnelly and his gang in August 1926, twelve new solitary confinement cells had been added to the north end of the old maximum-security building, bringing the total number of cells to eighteen. This was the largest number of punishment cells per capita of any prison in the nation.

A narrow corridor ran between the old and new sections. The new building, known as "the Hole," was used to administer a more severe form of punishment. The cells in the "Hole" were only three feet by eight feet, and the interior was very dark. There was a single electric light bulb in the corridor which was controlled by the guards. The cells themselves had no artificial lighting. Prisoners were sealed behind solid steel doors without bars. The only openings in each door were a few small air holes and a narrow slit through which food and water were passed.

The solid concrete building that housed the dungeon was ventilated by a small intake fan beside the only door to the outside. This fan was run only intermittently. The only other ventilation was a small ventilator in the roof of each cell.

The dungeon was very cold, as it was unheated and temperatures outside for the entire month of January 1929 never rose above freezing. At the beginning of Donnelly's stay, temperatures at night were down around zero degrees. The National Society for Penal Information said in 1929 that these cells were the worst seen in any institution in the United States.

Donnelly and his friends were left in the "Hole" and given only bread and water for at least ninety days. That was about all that a man could bear and still keep his sanity, although there were times when men were kept in this punishment section for as long as sixteen months.

Because this was Donnelly's third attempt to escape, Warden Wheeler declared that he was incorrigible. The warden was determined to never let this dangerous man back into the general population. When Donnelly was let out of the "Hole", he was moved across the hallway into the older part of the solitary confinement building, which had become known as "Old Siberia." For almost five years, Donnelly languished in this maximum-security cellblock.

Conditions in the older section were harsh but tolerable. In "Siberia," unruly inmates were simply left alone, separated from the rest of the population. They were basically ignored.

During this time, 1928-1933, the inmates in solitary confinement had to sleep on the cold, hard concrete floor with only a couple of cotton blankets to keep them warm. The metal beds had been removed after Donnelly and his friends made parts of them into weapons during the 1926 riot.

As before, the only illumination in each of the six cells in "Siberia" was provided by a few faint rays of daylight coming through a tiny hole in the ceiling. The cold air, rain, and snow also fell through these openings.

The meals served in "Siberia" were meager. Food was brought from the dining room and shoved to the inmates through a narrow opening in the exceptionally heavily barred steel doors. There was not much variety in the food served.

The penitentiary now had a sewer system. The prison sewer pipe ran under the dungeon building. Holes in the floors of the cells, opening directly into the sewer line served as toilets for the inmates.

Donnelly was mentally tough and able to endure the harsh conditions without breaking. He kept his sanity by engaging in Chinese and Hindu practices he'd read about earlier. He also maintained a strong physical condition by running in place and doing calisthenics in his small cell every single day. And he was not always alone. Due to the limited number of solitary confinement cells, sometimes a dozen other inmates were temporarily crammed into the tiny cell with Donnelly when there was a rash of misbehavior among the prison population.

Treatment of individual solitary confinement prisoners was up to the warden in charge. J. W. Wheeler stepped down as warden on April 1, 1931, replaced by R. E. Thomas. It is not known if Donnelly was ever let out of his dark cell for brief periods of exercise, or allowed to take an occasional shower, as some prisoners were. His treatment was entirely in the hands of the warden.

Idaho State Penitentiary Solitary Confinement Cell Block. Mike Donnelly spent twenty years in this prison. Five of those years were in solitary confinement in the "dungeon," located in the southwest corner of the prison compound. (Idaho State Historical Society, Boise, Idaho)

It was not until after George F. Rudd became warden at the prison on March 27, 1933, that fifty-one-year-old Donnelly was released from solitary confinement and brought out into the light. Warden Rudd believed in trying to rehabilitate all prisoners, even the most hardened. He gave Donnelly a job painting the prison walls, and this now mellow convict performed well.

Ira J. Taylor became warden at the prison on January 1, 1934. He was even more lenient toward the hardened criminals than his predecessor had been. When Warden Taylor observed that Donnelly continued to perform well in all areas, he gave this once-dangerous convict a trustee position as a janitor, with a considerable amount of freedom.

43

"Rehabilitated" Murderer Goes Free

DONNELLY'S GOAL WAS STILL TO GET OUT of prison. On July 20, 1937, he wrote a neatly hand-printed letter to prison authorities, asking their permission to appear before the July 1938 meeting of the Idaho State Board of Pardons. He stated that he wanted to ask the board for an early release.

Donnelly wrote, " . . . My intention is that I would ask for a reduction of time rather then an absolute pardon. And it would do me little good to claim or demand a right without first establishing the proper attitude with those who are part of the power that grants it. . . . It is not the opinion that I hold of myself so much that counts, but it is the opinion of organized society. Knowing these things, it is folly to persist in acting contrary to law and order. . . . I desire to make it known that I am willing to do the right thing."

The policy of the Idaho Board of Pardons was not to pardon or parole a prisoner before he completed his minimum sentence. But after the minimum required time, if a prisoner showed by his record and his actions that he was reformed and ready to accept the duties and responsibilities of living as a member of society, the board believed that all such prisoners—even those who had committed violent crimes—should be paroled and eventually pardoned.

Donnelly had completed his minimum sentence, so authorities helped him file an official "Notice of Intention to Apply for Pardon" with all of the required agencies throughout the state. When a notice of this application appeared in the *Northern Idaho News* in Sandpoint, Idaho, on June 3, 1938, objections started pouring in. Petitions containing the signatures of more than one hundred prominent citizens of Bonner County were sent to the Board of Pardons, asking that Donnelly's application for pardon be denied.

One petition was a scroll that, when unrolled, was three feet long and bore the signatures and seals of fifty-five Sandpoint businessmen and professionals. When the Board of Pardons met at the statehouse in Boise on Wednesday, July 6, 1938, Donnelly's application was denied.

By serving notice on August 25, 1938, of his intention to reapply for a pardon or commutation of sentence in 1939, Donnelly started the parole application process a second time. As required by law, a legal notice of his intentions once again appeared in the *Northern Idaho News* on September 2, 1938. This time Orville Crisp, son of the murder victim, responded with a personal letter to the board on behalf of the signers of the first petitions. He stated that Bonner County citizens would not be presenting a new petition after such a short period of time, but that the sentiments expressed in the first petitions had not changed. At the Board of Pardons meeting on July 5, 1939, Donnelly's application was again denied.

Donnelly applied for a pardon a third time in 1941. This time the Board of County Commissioners of Bonner County sent a letter to the Idaho State Board of Pardons, unanimously opposing any clemency for the convicted murderer. Dr. Malcolm P. McKinnon, Mayor of Sandpoint, and twenty-two other prominent citizens of Sandpoint sent a Western Union telegram to the Board, stating that "the sentiment of this entire community is against any pardon or parole granted now or at any future time to Mike Donnelly, murderer of Wm. Crisp of Hope, Idaho." The citizens of Hope also signed a petition requesting that the Board deny pardon or parole to Donnelly "now or any other time." The Board of Pardons again denied Donnelly's application.

Donnelly was unrelenting in his efforts to be released from prison. He repeated the application process again in 1942. Once more the Mayor of Sandpoint and the Bonner County Sheriff officially objected to granting Donnelly any sort of release from prison, but the intensity of the objections from northern Idaho was waning. At the same time, Donnelly was receiving support from Boise businessman James R. Compton, who had been helping prisoners gain their releases for more than twenty years.

Compton was the proprietor of Compton Transfer & Storage Company in Boise. He often hired ex-convicts to work for him. Compton lobbied for Donnelly's release throughout 1942. Besides being in the trucking and storage business, Compton was a retail coal dealer. He promised that, if Donnelly were released, he would keep him employed shoveling coal. Compton further promised that, if he could not keep Donnelly employed, he would share him with the other coal merchants who were also faced with a labor shortage due to World War II. Compton guaranteed to the Board of Pardons that he would personally be responsible for Donnelly's behavior on the outside.

The Idaho State Board of Pardons met on January 18, 1943, and decided to give Donnelly a conditional parole. On July 18, 1943, the prisoner was released into the custody of his new employer for a ninety-day preliminary trial. Then, on August 24, 1943, when the preliminary trial period had proved successful, he was granted a one-year conditional parole. The conditions were that he report to his parole officer, Walter H. Rhodes, at least every thirty days, that he remain in the employ of J. R. Compton, that he remain at all times within Ada County, Idaho, and that he specifically never go back to Bonner County, Idaho. After serving almost twenty years of his life sentence in the Idaho State Penitentiary, fifty-nine-year-old Mike Donnelly was out of jail again.

Jim Compton set Donnelly up in a tiny house at 214 South Sixth Street—between Grove and Front Streets—for which Donnelly paid rent of ten dollars per month. The house was less than a block away from the coal yard where he worked and only five blocks from Compton's main office and warehouse.

Donnelly earned about two hundred dollars per month shoveling coal out of railroad cars into storage bins. From time to time, when Compton's business was slow, Donnelly worked for the Worthington & Coffin Coal Company at 318 North Eighth Street. Both coal yards were in Boise, just north of the Boise River.

44

Off to Oregon

AT THE END OF HIS FIRST YEAR on parole, Donnelly received glowing reports in his file from James R. Compton, from coal merchants Samuel W. Worthington and Edward H. Coffin, and from Parole Officer W. H. Rhodes. At a meeting held on July 8, 1944, Idaho Governor Clarence A. Bottolfsen, who was also the chairman of the Board of Pardons, signed an order granting Mike Donnelly an absolute pardon, effective on July 18, 1944. Donnelly was a free man in every state except Washington, where he was still wanted for violating the conditions of his parole in 1923.

Donnelly's friends in Boise petitioned the Washington State Board of Pardons to drop the parole violation charges still pending against him there. The board's response was that they did not know of any legal way for them to do that, and they were not interested in pursuing the matter. Officials did say, however, that it was not likely that the State of Washington would ever come after Donnelly and seek extradition for the charge of parole violation.

After receiving his pardon, Donnelly went to work for the McCaslinn Lumber Company at 2615 Fairview Avenue in Boise. The very large lumberyard was on the south side of Fairview Avenue where it intersected South 27th Street and U. S. Highway 30. Besides lumber, shingles, flooring, etc., McCaslinn sold "Utah King" coal. Donnelly worked in the coal bins at the south end of the yard on a sidetrack of the Oregon Short Line Railroad until the summer of 1947.

After adjusting to the idea that he was a free man, he began feeling too confined in the city. He longed for the wilds of the evergreen forests of the Pacific Northwest. He could not return to Washington nor to North Idaho, but the forests of Oregon were only three hundred miles due west of Boise. In the summer of 1947, he quit his job, packed up his meager belongings, and moved to Eugene, Oregon.

In Oregon Donnelly did odd jobs on a couple of ranches near Eugene. When he was not working and living on a ranch, he earned a little money by salvaging scrap metal and selling it to local junk dealers. He camped out in the bush and supplemented his diet with whatever wild fruits and berries were ripening at the time. His hobby was prospecting for gold and silver in the hills.

Donnelly had been in Eugene for a few months when he was arrested for vagrancy in the fall of 1947. He was caught picking things out of the Eugene city dump, a violation of a city ordinance. After serving time in jail for vagrancy, Donnelly decided that it was time to get out of town. He traveled east across the Cascade Mountains to Redmond, Oregon, in Deschutes County.

Donnelly had paid into Social Security while working in Boise, so he was eligible to draw a small pension after his sixty-fifth birthday in April 1948. He applied for and received the minimum benefit of ten dollars per month. While in Redmond, Donnelly continued to supplement his income by salvaging junk from the city dump and other places. He picked up aluminum, copper, tin, and other metals that he could sell.

Donnelly teamed up with a new partner, forty-one-year-old Lee Marcus Russum, who helped him in his junk-dealing enterprise. The pair camped in a tent in the desert about a quarter-mile east of the Redmond city limits.

45

The End of the Road

IT SEEMS THAT THE LURE OF EASY MONEY and the excitement of a life of crime were too much for this habitual offender to resist. In the summer of 1950, Donnelly and his new sidekick started burglarizing and robbing warehouses in and around Redmond. As he typically did, Donnelly had a younger, somewhat gullible partner whom he could use as a scapegoat if necessary.

The Deschutes County Prosecutor wanted to file charges against the pair as early as August first, but he did not have enough evidence for a conviction. Two more warehouses—the Fred Hodecker Potato Company and the Baker Feed Company—were hit on Monday night, August 28, in what the police described as "amateurish," unsuccessful attempts to open the companies' safes. It appears that in his old age, Donnelly was trying to add a new dimension to his career—safecracking.

In early October 1950, Donnelly and Russum broke into a City of Redmond storage building at Roberts Field, the former military airbase in Redmond, not far from their camp in the desert. They stole a large quantity of copper service pipe valued at around four hundred dollars, then used an old car to haul the pipe back to their camp, where they buried it.

A Redmond city employee, Taylor McClay, discovered the theft and called his boss, City Superintendent John Berning. Redmond Chief of Police John McKelvey and Deschutes County Sheriff C. L. McCauley were called in to investigate. The Oregon State Police were also called, and State Trooper W. P. Simpson was put on the case. This trio of law enforcement officers found footprints at the scene of the burglary that were later matched to the two suspects. They also found automobile tire tracks which led them to the outlaws' camp in the desert. A search of the camp resulted in the discovery of the buried copper pipe. The county prosecutor finally had the evidence that he wanted. Donnelly and Russum were arrested on October 10 and taken to the Redmond City Jail.

The two men were charged with grand larceny. On October 21 they were transferred to the Deschutes County Jail in Bend, Oregon, to await trial. Public defenders were appointed for each man. Attorney Harry English of Bend defended Donnelly and Robert H. Foley of Bend defended Russum.

Donnelly's trial was held in circuit court in Bend on Tuesday, November 28, 1950. His attorney allowed him to take the witness stand, thus opening the door for Assistant District Attorney Thomas Boeke to introduce Donnelly's past murder convictions into evidence. After only a short deliberation, the jury convicted Donnelly of grand larceny. Russum's trial was held the next day. He, too, was convicted of grand larceny. At eleven a.m., Friday, December 1, Circuit Judge Ralph Hamilton gave both men the maximum sentence for larceny allowed by Oregon law—ten years in the state penitentiary.

Oregon State Penitentiary at Salem, Oregon, in 1947. Sixty-eight-year-old Mike Donnelly was received at this prison on December 4, 1950. He was sentenced to ten years for larceny. (Salem Public Library)

Sheriff McCauley and Redmond Police Chief McKelvey escorted Donnelly and Russum to the State Penitentiary in Salem, Oregon, on Monday, December 4, 1950. After seven years of freedom, sixty-eight-year-old Donnelly was once more behind bars—a place where he had spent most of his adult life. He was designated as Oregon State Penitentiary Inmate No. 21148.

Because of his past history of escape, Donnelly was placed under close supervision at the Oregon penitentiary and not given much freedom. Oregon prison records described him as being in excellent physical condition for his age. Allowed to have a job in the "vegetable room" of the prison kitchen, he was happy with his assignment and caused no trouble. He had spent so much of his life locked up that he adjusted easily to the prison routine.

Donnelly was first eligible for parole from the Oregon prison in April 1954, after a little more than three years in prison. On May 8, 1954, he applied for release, but parole was denied at that time. The board set a "good time date" of August 4, 1957. That meant that if Donnelly did not get into trouble before that date, he would probably be set free. He continued to behave himself in prison and was given an unconditional early release on July 1, 1957, after serving

Mike Donnelly, Age 72. Photo taken at the Oregon State Penitentiary on May 12, 1954. (Oregon Department of Corrections)

almost six and a half years of his ten-year sentence. He was no longer considered a menace to society.

When released from the Oregon State Penitentiary at age seventy-four, Donnelly moved back to Idaho. In 1959 he was living in Corwin Apartment Building No. 2 at 1215 South First Street in Nampa, where he shared a room with a man named Everett Gould. Donnelly's last Nampa post office address was Route 1. He celebrated his eightieth birthday at his home in Nampa on April 3, 1963.

After all of the crime and gun play, and after all of the time in jail that Donnelly experienced during his lifetime, he managed to die a free man. He died of natural causes at the ripe old age of eighty. This colorful outlaw passed into history in Nampa on Friday, August 23, 1963. The Shepherd Mortuary held graveside services for him at Koherlawn Cemetery in Nampa on Thursday, August 29, but few people came to say farewell.

Sources of the Story

NEWSPAPERS

Bellingham Herald, The; Whatcom County, Washington.

Bend Bulletin, The; Bend, Deschutes County, Oregon.

Boise Capital News; Boise, Ada County, Idaho.

Bonners Ferry Herald; weekly; Bonners Ferry, Boundary County, Idaho.

Bourbon News, The; Paris, Bourbon County, Kentucky.

Chehalis Bee-Nugget, The; Chehalis, Lewis County, Washington.

Central Record, The; Lancaster, Garrard County, Kentucky.

Centralia News-Examiner; Centralia, Lewis County, Washington.

Coeur d'Alene Press, The; Coeur d'Alene, Kootenai County, Idaho.

Daily Missoulian, The; Missoula, Missoula County, Montana.

Daily Chronicle-Examiner; Centralia, Lewis County, Washington.

Daily Ledger, The; Tacoma, Pierce County, Washington.

Evening and Sunday Morning Bulletin; Walla Walla, Walla Walla County, Washington.

Dillon Examiner; weekly; Dillon, Beaverhead County, Montana.

Dillon Tribune; weekly; Dillon, Beaverhead County, Montana.

Evening Capital News; Boise, Ada County, Idaho.

Everett Daily Herald, The; Everett, Snohomish County, Washington.

Hood River Glacier; Hood River, Hood River County, Oregon.

Hood River News, The; Hood River, Hood River County, Oregon.

Idaho Daily Statesman; Boise, Ada County, Idaho.

Idaho Free Press; Nampa, Canyon County, Idaho.

Monroe Monitor-Transcript; Monroe, Snohomish County, Washington.

Morning Reveille, The; Bellingham, Whatcom County, Washington.

Northern Idaho News; weekly; Sandpoint, Bonner County, Idaho.

Pend Oreille Review, The; weekly; Sandpoint, Bonner County, Idaho.

Plainsman, The; weekly; Plains, Sanders County, Montana.

Post-Intelligencer, The; Seattle, King County, Washington.

Priest River Times; weekly; Priest River, Bonner County, Idaho.

Redmond Spokesman, The; Redmond, Deschutes County, Oregon.

Seattle Daily Times, The; Seattle, King County, Washington.

Skagit County Times, The; weekly; Sedro-Woolley, Skagit County, Washington.

Snohomish County Tribune; Snohomish, Snohomish County, Washington.

Spokane Daily Chronicle; Spokane, Spokane County, Washington.

Spokesman-Review, The; Spokane, Spokane County, Washington.

Sultan Star, The; Sultan, Snohomish County, Washington.

Tacoma Tribune, The; Tacoma, Pierce County, Washington.

Walla Walla Union; Walla Walla, Walla Walla County, Washington.

CRIMINAL CASE AND INMATE FILES

Circuit Court Criminal Case File No. 5953-1912, Bourbon County, Commonwealth of Kentucky vs. Noah Arnold, File Box 32, Kentucky Dept. for Libraries and Archives, 300 Coffee Tree Rd., Frankfort, Kentucky 40602.

Criminal Case File No. 22944, "Ford, Robert" (Arnold, Noah), Microfilm Reel #34D, Pierce County Clerk, 930 Tacoma Ave. S., Tacoma, Washington 98402.

Inmate File No. 3301, Idaho State Penitentiary, "Arnold, Noah", File Box 1025, A06D01F, Idaho State Historical Society Library and Archives, 450 N. 4th Street, Boise, Idaho 83702.

Inmate File No. 3302, Idaho State Penitentiary, "Donnelly, Mike", Idaho State Historical Society Library and Archives, 450 N. 4th Street, Boise, Idaho 83702.

Inmate File No. 21148, Oregon State Penitentiary, "Donnelly, Mike", Oregon Department of Corrections, P.O. Box 5670, Wilsonville, Oregon 97070.

Inmate File No. 2197, Washington State Reformatory in Monroe, Washington, "Ford, Robert" (Arnold, Noah), Washington State Archives & Records, P.O. Box 40238, Olympia, Washington 98504.

Inmate File No. 8432, Washington State Penitentiary, "Arnold, Noah", Washington State Archives & Records, P.O. Box 40238, Olympia, Washington 98504-0238.

Inmate File No. 6120, Washington State Penitentiary, "Donnelly, Mike", Washington State Archives & Records, P.O. Box 40238, Olympia, Washington 98504-0238.

"Register of Prisoners Confined in the County Jail of Bonneville County, Idaho, 1911," pages 6-7, Museum of Idaho Archives, 200 N. Eastern Ave., Idaho Falls, Idaho 83402.

PUBLICATIONS AND PERIODICALS

King, Max C., "Mike Donnelly: His Escapades Are Remembered In Snohomish, Sultan and Acme", *Charmed Land Magazine of The Seattle Sunday Times*, Seattle, Washington, March 10, 1963, pages 12-13.

Kyle, Irene (Crisp), "Early Hope Recollections" [written in 1990], *Beautiful Bonner History and Memories, Vol. II*, Bonner County Historical Society, Inc., Sandpoint, Idaho, 2000, page 171.

Royer, Marie Hamel, "Galbraith-Stevens Tragedy", *The Saxon Story: Early Pioneers on the South Fork*, Whatcom County Historical

Society, Bellingham, Washington, pages 267-268.

Sevy, Jil M., "Old Idaho Penitentiary State Historical Site Walking Tour Guide," revised 2002, Idaho State Historical Society, 2445 Old Penitentiary Rd., Boise, Idaho 83712.

THE AUTHOR GRATEFULLY ACKNOWLEDGES THE FOLLOWING INSTITUTIONS AND ORGANIZATIONS FOR THEIR ASSISTANCE IN LOCATING INFORMA-TION FOR THE STORY:

Bonner County Historical Society, 611 S. Ella Avenue, Sandpoint, Idaho 83864.

Bonneville County Historical Society, 200 N. Eastern Avenue, Idaho Falls, Idaho 83402.

Bourbon County Library, 701 High Street, Paris, Kentucky, 40361.

Canyon County Historical Society, 1200 Front Street, Nampa, Idaho 83651.

Deschutes County Historical Society, 129 NW Idaho Avenue, Bend, Oregon 97701.

Everett Public Library, Northwest Room, 2702 Hoyt Avenue, Everett, Washington, 98201-3556.

Hood River County Library, 502 State Street, Hood River, Oregon 97031.

Idaho State Historical Society Library and Archives, 450 N. 4th Street, Boise, Idaho 83702.

Kentucky Department for Libraries and Archives, Public Records Division, P.O. Box 537, Frankfort, Kentucky, 40602.

Lewis County Historical Museum, 599 NW Front Way, Chehalis, Washington 98532.

Missoula Public Library, 301 E. Main, Missoula, Montana 59802-4799.

Montana Historical Society Library, P.O. Box 201201, Helena, Montana 59620-1201.

Plains Public Library District, 108 W. Railroad, Plains, Montana 59859.

Redmond Public Library, 827 SW Deschutes Avenue, Redmond, Oregon 97756.

Skagit River Journal of History & Folklore, 810 Central Avenue, Sedro-Woolley, Washington 98284.

Snohomish Historical Society, P.O. Box 174, Snohomish, Washington 98291-0174.

Sno-Isle Regional Library, 319 Main Street, Suite 100, Sultan, Washington 98294.

Spokane Public Library, Northwest Room, 906 W. Main Avenue, Spokane, Washington 99201.

Tacoma Public Library, 1102 Tacoma Avenue S., Tacoma, Washington 98402-2098.

Washington State Library, 6880 Capitol Boulevard. S., Olympia, Washington 98501-5513.

Whatcom Museum of History & Art, 121 Prospect Street, Bellingham, Washington 98225.

Index